Agricultural Finance and Marketing in India

Agricultural Finance and Marketing in India

Makarand Upadhyaya
Associate Professor,
Department of Management and Marketing,
College of Business Administration,
University of Bahrain, Bahrain

New Century Publications
New Delhi, India

NEW CENTURY PUBLICATIONS
4852 / 24, 1st Floor,
Ansari Road, Daryaganj,
New Delhi – 110 002 (India)

Tel.: 011-4101 7798; 4358 7398; 98112 66355
E-mail: info@newcenturypublications.com

www.newcenturypublications.com

Editorial office:
4800 / 24, Bharat Ram Road,
Ansari Road, Daryaganj,
New Delhi – 110 002

First Published: **2022**

ISBN: **978-81-7708-537-2**

Published by New Century Publications and printed at Milan Enterprises, New Delhi.

Designs: Patch Creative Unit, New Delhi.

PRINTED IN INDIA

About the Book

Agricultural production in India depends upon millions of small farmers. Agricultural methods and techniques used by them are crucial for raising yields per hectare. Because of inadequate financial resources and absence of timely credit facilities at reasonable rates, many of the farmers, even though otherwise willing, are unable to go in for improved seeds, plant protection measures and tools and implements. It is, therefore, important that financial requirements of the farmers are adequately met.

Disposal of the produce after harvest and the return obtained, have a significant effect on production and on the welfare of the cultivators. Marketing is the last link in the chain of production process. An efficient marketing system which ensures reasonable return to the producers is essential to induce them to produce more. Production in agriculture being seasonal, the crop is harvested during a short period and consumed gradually. In the absence of staying power of a large number of small farmers, they compete with each other and the markets witness conditions of occasional glut and scarcity. Moreover, sale of agricultural produce involves a number of functions such as assembling, storing, grading, standardising, transporting and financing of the produce and negotiating sale. All this calls for adequate credit facilities for the farmers and an efficient and remunerative system of marketing of agricultural produce.

This book explains and examines various aspects of agricultural finance and marketing in India. It contains 15 chapters which have been organized into 3 parts.

Part I (chapters 1 and 2) is titled Introduction to Indian Agriculture. It provides an overview of agricultural finance, marketing and commerce during British rule. Besides, it gives a brief introduction of the present state of agricultural sector in India.

Part II (chapters 3 to 8) is titled Agricultural Finance. It discusses credit needs and sources of Indian farmers, rural co-operative credit institutions, regional rural banks (RRBs), micro finance and self-help groups (SHGs), kisan credit cards (KCCs) and farm loan waivers.

Part III (chapters 9 to 15) is titled Agricultural Marketing and Commerce. It deals with importance and requirements of a sound agricultural marketing system, present system of agricultural marketing, national agriculture market (e-NAM), minimum support prices (MSP), food stocks, food subsidy, public distribution system (PDS), agricultural exports and imports, and the three controversial farm laws (now repealed).

About the Author

Dr. Makarand Upadhyaya is currently an Associate Professor, Department of Management and Marketing, College of Business Administration, University of Bahrain, Bahrain. An alumnus of the University of Rajasthan, Jaipur, India, Dr. Upadhyaya achieved his Ph.D in 2010. He also holds an MBA, PGDPM and PGDCA from Vikram University, Ujjain, India.

Armed with over 25 years of combined experience in industry and academia, he was awarded the Faculty Distinguished Scholarship Award in 2007 by the Research Council, India.

His areas of research fall within the domains of consumer behaviour and strategic board leadership. He has also authored several books, including:

- Digital Marketing
- Marketing Lessons: A Case Study Approach
- Leadership: Find Your Way to Lead
- 75 Years of Industrial, Infrastructural and Logistics Development in India: 1947-48 to 2021-22
- Public-Private-Partnership (PPP) and Economic Development: Theory and Recent Experiences
- Marketing Management: Concepts, Theories and Practices
- Marketing Strategies and Management: Sector Analysis
- Media Planning: Impact of TV Advertisements on Children
- Generation, Transmission and Switchgear

Dr. Upadhyaya has over 100 research papers published in various international journals, while also being the chair and a member of various committees and advisory boards on business strategies and economic growth. He has conducted more than 40 training and development sessions on client relationships, behavioural aspects of the overseas market, stress management, interpersonal skills, and team building, for senior management across many multinational companies. He is a keen enthusiast of sports and has been a national player in basketball and cricket during his younger days.

Contents

Preface

Agricultural sector occupies a key position in the Indian economy. According to the Annual Report of the Ministry of Agriculture and Farmers' Welfare, 2020-21, "Agriculture plays a vital role in India's economy. 54.6 percent of the total workforce is engaged in agriculture and allied sector activities and accounts for 17.8 percent of the country's gross value added (GVA) for the year 2019-20 (at current prices)".

Agriculture being a state subject, the bulk of public investment in agriculture takes place at the level of State Governments and the Central Government supports the states as a catalyst. The nodal agency for development of agriculture in India is the Ministry of Agriculture and Farmers Welfare, Government of India.

Agricultural products like cereals (mainly rice), tea, coffee, cashew, spices, tobacco and leather are important items of India's exports and hence foreign exchange earnings.

There is inter-dependence between agriculture and industry. The development of the agricultural sector depends, to a large extent, on such core industries as power, petroleum, fertilisers, insecticides and agricultural machinery. Industry, on the other hand, depends on agriculture for the supply of raw material for agro-based industries including textiles, cigarettes, jute, sugar, paper, processed foodstuffs and *vanaspati*.

Although Indian agriculture is way back compared to the levels in developed countries, some notable developments have occurred over the last 75 years. Large areas which suffered from repeated failures of rainfall have received irrigation, new crops have come to occupy a significant position in the country's production and trade, agricultural and the industrial economies now exert a powerful influence on one another, problems of rural indebtedness and the exploitative practices of the village moneylenders are much less, and finally there is visible in the countryside an awakening and a desire for better standard of living.

Agricultural production in India depends upon millions of small farmers. It is the intensity of their effort and the efficiency of their technique that will help in raising yields per hectare. Because of inadequate financial resources and absence of timely credit facilities at reasonable rates, many of the farmers, even though otherwise willing, are unable to go in for improved seeds and manures or to introduce better methods or techniques. It is, therefore, of the utmost importance that the financial requirements of the farmers are adequately met.

Need for agricultural credit arises because modern farm technology is costly and the personal resources of the farmers are inadequate. Provision of agricultural credit, as an input, is essential for widespread use of improved agricultural methods.

Fortunately, micro credit, routed through self-help groups (SHGs), has emerged as a visible credit channel to the poor as their access to conventional credit channels is constrained by the requirement of collateral and high transaction cost.

Disposal of the produce after harvest and the return obtained have a significant effect on production and on the welfare of the cultivator. Marketing is the last link in the chain of production process. An efficient marketing system which ensures reasonable return to the producers is essential to induce them to produce more. Production in agriculture being seasonal, the crop is harvested during a short period and consumed gradually. In the absence of staying power of a large number of small farmers, they compete with each other and the markets witness conditions of occasional glut and scarcity. Moreover, sale of agricultural produce involves a number of functions such as assembling, storing, grading, standardising, transporting and financing the produce and negotiating sale.

All this calls for adequate credit facilities for the farmers and an efficient and remunerative system of marketing of agricultural produce.

Bahrain **Makarand Upadhyaya**
July 2022

Abbreviations/Acronyms

AIF	Agriculture Infrastructure Fund
AMFFRI	Agricultural Marketing and Farmer Friendly Reforms Index
APEDA	Agricultural and Processed Food Products Export Development Authority
APL	Above Poverty Line
APMC	Agricultural Produce Marketing Committee
ARC	Agricultural Refinance Corporation
ARDC	Agricultural Refinance and Development Corporation
BC	Business Correspondent
BIRD	Bankers Institute of Rural Development
BPL	Below Poverty Line
CACP	Commission for Agricultural Costs and Prices
CCBs	Central Co-operative Banks
CCEA	Cabinet Committee on Economic Affairs
CCS	Co-operative Credit Structure
CIP	Central Issue Price
CRAFICARD	Committee to Review Arrangements for Institutional Credit for Agriculture and Rural Development
CSMS	Core Subsidy Management System
CWC	Central Warehousing Corporation
DBT	Direct Benefit Transfer
DMI	Directorate of Marketing and Inspection
EC Act	Essential Commodities Act
e-NAM	National Agriculture Market
FCI	Food Corporation of India
FMC	Forward Markets Commission
FPOs	Farmer Producer Organizations
FPS	Fair Price Shop
GDP	Gross Domestic Product
GrAMs	Gramin Agricultural Markets
GVA	Gross Value Added

HYV	High Yield Variety
IRDP	Integrated Rural Development Programme
IT	Information Technology
JLG	Joint Liability Group
KCCs	Kisan Credit Cards
LDCs	Less Developed Countries
MFIs	Micro Finance Institutions
MGNREGA	Mahatma Gandhi National Rural Employment Guarantee Act
MIS	Market Intervention Scheme
MSP	Minimum Support Price
NABARD	National Bank for Agriculture and Rural Development
NAFED	National Agricultural Co-operative Marketing Federation
NCAER	National Council of Applied Economic Research
NDDB	National Dairy Development Board
NFSA	National Food Security Act
NGOs	Non-governmental Organizations
NIAM	National Institute of Agricultural Marketing
NIC	National Informatics Centre
NITI Aayog	National Institution for Transforming India
ONORC	One Nation One Ration Card
OTS	One Time Settlement
PACS	Primary Agricultural Credit Society
PCARDBs	Primary Co-operative Agriculture and Rural Development Banks
PDS	Public Distribution System
PFEPC	Processed Food Export Promotion Council
PGDABM	Post-graduate Diploma in Agri-Business Management
PMGKAY	Pradhan Mantri Garib Kalyan Anna Yojana
PPP	Public-Private-Partnership
RBI	Reserve Bank of India
RFA	Revolving Fund Assistance

RKCCs	RuPay ATM-cum-Debit Kisan Credit Cards
RRBs	Regional Rural Banks
SAA	Service Area Approach
SACP	Special Agricultural Credit Plan
SCARDBs	State Co-operative Agriculture and Rural Development Banks
SCB	State Co-operative Bank
SFAC	Small Farmers Agri-business Consortium
SHG	Self-help Group
SSIs	Small-scale Industries
SWCs	State Warehousing Corporations
TPDS	Targeted Public Distribution System
UAM	Unified Agriculture Marketing
UCBs	Urban Co-operative Banks
UTs	Union Territories
WTO	World Trade Organization

Part I
Introduction to Indian Agriculture

1

Agricultural Finance, Marketing and Commerce during British Rule

Prior to Independence in 1947, India was a dependency of the United Kingdom and consisted of British India, and the Princely States. It encompassed the entire area which now forms the four countries of India, Pakistan, Myanmar (formerly Burma), and Bangladesh. The British came to India as merchants in the middle of the 17th century. After gaining foothold on the coastline, they spread to every corner of the Indian peninsula. They gained political supremacy around the middle of the 18th century. After winning the Battle of Plassey in 1757 and the Battle of Buxer in 1764, they established themselves firmly as the rulers of India and ruled it till 1947 to sub-serve their economic interests. At the time of the arrival of the British, Indian economy was, by and large, self-sufficient, possessing a fine balance between agriculture and industry.

India inherited a dismal economy from the British rulers at the time of Independence. Indian agriculture was traditional and stagnant in every respect. It was characterized by feudal land relations, primitive technology, and the resultant low productivity per hectare. The first task of Indian Government in the immediate post-Independence period was, therefore, to initiate growth process in agriculture on modern lines. Modernization of agriculture was required both in terms of technological and institutional changes. Abolition of intermediaries in agriculture, like *zamindars* and *jagirdars*, was accomplished soon after Independence.

1.1 Agricultural Finance

Provision of sufficient and timely credit at fair rates of interest is considered as an integral part of agricultural development strategy. Need for agricultural credit arises because personal resources of the farmers are inadequate. Provision of agricultural credit, as an input, is essential for widespread use of improved agricultural methods.

1.1.1 Role of Moneylenders: Long before the British acquired control, the rulers of the day were accustomed to grant loans to the cultivators of the soil. This system was continued by the early British administrators, and in 1793 various regulations were issued providing for *taccavi* advances to proprietors, farmers, subordinate tenants and *ryots* for embankments, tanks, watercourses etc. These were followed by a series of Acts which, with much improvement, were later represented by the Land Improvement Loans Act of 1883 and the Agriculturists Loans Act of 1884 and the Rules framed thereunder.

Money-lending is one of the oldest professions in India. Prior to Independence, there were two types of moneylenders in rural areas: (a) agriculturist moneylenders who carried on the business of money lending along with farming, and (b) professional moneylenders whose only occupation was money lending.

Moneylenders usually charged higher rates from poorer borrowers than from less poor ones. While moneylenders were often demonized and accused of usury, their services were convenient and fast, and they could be flexible when borrowers ran into problems. Moneylenders were popular because, unlike government agencies, they gave credit for every purpose. They were easily approachable by the credit seekers and there were not many formalities in transacting a loan. Borrowers were prepared to pay high interest rates for services like quick loan disbursement, confidentiality and flexible repayment schedules. In normal times, the village moneylender seems to have met the normal needs, but in times of severe drought or widespread calamity, his resources proved unequal to the strain upon them.

However, the malpractices adopted by the moneylenders to exploit the needy farmers cannot be overlooked. These malpractices pertained to charging of high rate of interest and adopting unfair means in the maintenance of accounts. Perhaps influenced by traditional Western views about usury, the role of the traditional moneylender was subject to much criticism.

Till Independence in 1947, money lenders and the landlords were the principal sources of rural credit. Over the years, the operations of moneylenders have declined in view of debt relief legislations, the system of licensing moneylenders and restrictions on the use and transfer of land as security. Similarly, the abolition of all privileged tenures, both in zamindari and ryotwari areas, has discouraged investment by the landlords and larger cultivators.

Historically, moneylenders have played a significant role in meeting the credit needs of the rural producers. With stringent laws against money lending and the phenomenal growth of the formal credit delivery system, it was thought that money lenders would soon be out of business. Instead they have been in the business of lending in several disguises.

Although the relative importance of moneylenders has declined over the years, they are still an important source of credit for rural people, particularly small farmers and the artisans.

1.1.2 Co-operative Credit Societies Act, 1904: The agricultural conditions and absence of institutional arrangements to provide finance to agriculturists during the latter part of the 19th century led to mounting distress and discontent. The Famine Commission of 1880 and 20 years later, the Famine Commission 1901 both highlighted the deep indebtedness of the Indian farmer, resulting in many cases in his land passing into the possession of the money lending classes. The Deccan Riots and the prevailing environment of discontent resulted in the government taking various initiatives but the legislative measures did not substantially improve the situation.

In 1901, the Famine Commission recommended the establishment of Rural Agricultural Banks through the establishment of Mutual Credit Associations, and such steps as were taken by the Government of North Western Provinces and Oudh. The underlying idea of a number of persons combining together was the voluntary creation of a new and valuable security. A strong association competent to offer guarantees and advantages of lending to groups instead of individuals were major advantages.

Taking cognizance of these developments and to provide a legal basis for co-operative societies, the Edward Law Committee was appointed by the Government to examine and recommend a course of action. Based on the recommendations of this Committee, the Co-operative Credit Societies Act was enacted on March 25, 1904. The Act was restricted to credit co-operatives. By 1911, there were 5,300 societies in existence with a membership of over 3 lakh.

The Act of 1904 provided for constitution of societies, eligibility for membership, registration, liabilities on members, disposal of profits, shares and interests of members, privileges of societies, claims against members, audit, inspection and enquiry, dissolution, exemption from taxation and rule making power. All other operational and managerial issues were left to the local governments, namely to formulate suitable rules and model bye-laws of the co-operative societies. The institution of the Registrar, visualized as a special official mechanism to be manned by officers with special training and appropriate attitudinal traits to prompt and catalyze co-operative development was the result of the Act of 1904.

The Act of 1904 was amended in 1912 to permit the formation of societies for purposes other than credit. As a result, societies for a variety of purposes began to be organized. This process of diversification was, however, slow in its pace. When individualism was the order of the day, co-operation represented a defensive act of association on the part of individual citizens. However, with the adoption of the principle of social regulation, the co-operative societies, which from their commencement in India have been socially sponsored and supported, came to occupy a more positive role.

1.1.3 Maclagen Committee on Co-operation (1914): The First World War adversely affected the growth of co-operatives. Although member deposits in co-operatives increased sharply, the War affected the exports and prices of cash crops adversely, resulting in increased overdues of loans of primary agricultural societies. To take stock of the situation, a Committee on Co-operation under Sir Edward Maclagen was appointed by the Government in October 1914, to study the state of co-operatives and make recommendations for the future. The Committee's recommendations basically related to credit co-operatives. It recommended building up a strong three-tier structure in every province with primaries at the base, the Central Co-operative Banks at the middle-tier and the Provincial Co-operative Bank at the apex, basically to provide short-term and medium-term finance. Considerable emphasis was laid on ensuring the co-operative character of these institutions and training and member education, including training of the Registrar and his staff.

The Committee recommended as follows:

1. Numbering not less than 10, individuals can combine together as they are unable to obtain credit individually.
2. Real security not to consist of material assets of members, but their ability and desire to use credit productively and to repay loans out of profits made.
3. Societies to be co-operative and business like, small in size.
4. One vote per member, transparency of business transactions, development of thrift and obtaining maximum capital from savings.
5. Period of the loan be fixed based on purpose of loan and the circumstances of the borrower.
6. Rates of interest to be initially substantial, although lower than that on credit from moneylenders.
7. Efforts to be made to increase deposits both from members and non-members.
8. Maximum borrowing limit of the society be fixed annually.
9. Obtaining share capital in instalments for inculcating thrift and providing capital.

10. Interest rates not to be reduced until reserve funds reach substantial figure.
11. Frequent audit by higher co-operative institutions with Government Audit once in 2 or 3 years, with cost being met by the societies.
12. Registrar to ensure supervision and control of primary societies without assuming detailed direction.

Under the Government of India Act, 1919, Co-operation as a subject was transferred to the provinces. The Bombay Co-operative Societies Act of 1925, the first provincial Act to be passed, among others, introduced the principle of one-man one-vote.

1.1.4 Recommendations of Royal Commission on Agriculture (RCA), 1928: The agricultural credit scenario was a matter of concern and various committees looked into the problems of co-operative banks in various provinces. RCA also reviewed the co-operative sector and among others recommended the setting up of land mortgage banks.

RCA, appointed to make recommendations for improvement of agriculture and promotion of welfare and prosperity of the rural population, submitted its report in April 1928. Main recommendations of RCA as regards co-operatives were as under:

1. Main activities of the co-operative movement must continue to be directed to expansion of the rural credit system.
2. Need for members' education was stressed.
3. Role of the Registrar to be not merely a registering officer, but to provide supervision, assistance, counsel and control.
4. To ensure continuity, Registrar not to be transferred for a minimum period of 5 years.
5. More Government contribution in backward tracts and for certain activities such as irrigation, consolidation of land holdings etc.
6. Establishment of land mortgage banks with guarantee of interest on its debentures by Government to meet the requirements of the cultivator other than small needs.
7. Single purpose co-operatives, by and large, favoured.

Need for extension of co-operative principles in fields other than co-operative credit, e.g. co-operative input and sale societies.

Both agricultural and non-agricultural societies were organized, but most of them faced difficulties in operation as a result of opposition by private marketing agencies and also the inexperience of their office bearers. This focused attention on strengthening of co-operative institutes and unions for education and training. A prominent development of this time was the setting up of the All India Association of Co-operative Institutes in 1929.

1.1.5 Co-operative Planning Committee (1945): Following the recommendations of the 14th Conference of Registrars of Co-operative Societies held in 1944, the Co-operative Planning Committee (Chairman: R.G. Saraiya) was constituted in January 1945 to draw up a plan of co-operative development in the country. It submitted its report in November 1945. The Committee felt that supply of credit touches only one aspect of the life of the cultivator and the activities of primary co-operative societies should be so extended as to cover the whole of his life. The main recommendations of the Committee were as under:

1. Multi-purpose society should serve as a centre for general economic improvement. Apart from financing crop production, it should act as an agent for sale of produce to the nearest co-operative marketing organization; serve as milk collecting station for the nearest dairy and provision of veterinary services; maintain agriculture machinery to be jointly used by members and encourage subsidiary occupations by its members.
2. Membership of such societies should be a minimum of 50 and confined to an area of operation, which would ensure adequate business as well as efficient supervision and control.
3. Except in cases where unlimited liability has been successful, the society should be one of limited liability.
4. Linking of agricultural credit with marketing. Credit societies

should give loans on the condition that the borrowing member would sell the marketable surplus through his primary society to the nearest marketing society of the area.

The Committee also dealt in detail with co-operatives in the areas of animal husbandry and fisheries, agricultural marketing and processing, agricultural credit, labour and civil construction, consumers, urban credit, housing societies, women and co-operation, co-operative administration and education training and research.

1.1.6 Other Developments: The setting up of the Reserve Bank of India (RBI) in 1934 was a major development in the thrust for agricultural credit. The Reserve Bank of India Act, 1934 itself required the RBI to set up an Agricultural Credit Department. As co-operatives were to be channels for rural development, with the establishment of popularly elected governments in 1935, programmes were drawn up in which rural indebtedness received priority. The Mehta Committee appointed in 1937 specifically recommended reorganization of Co-operative Credit Societies as multi-purpose co-operatives.

The Second World War boosted the prices of agricultural commodities leading to increased returns to farmers and consequently reduction in over-dues to the co-operatives. To counter shortages of essential commodities for domestic consumption as well as raw materials, the Government resorted to procurement of commodities from producers and rationing, for which it decided to utilize the co-operatives. This provided a momentum to the growth of multi-purpose co-operatives.

The period between 1939 and 1945 provided a further stimulus to the growth of the urban co-operative credit structure. Many societies had started banking functions and had grown in size and operations over a period of time, with substantial diversification of activities.

1.2 Agricultural Marketing

Disposal of the produce after harvest and the return obtained have a significant effect on production and on the welfare of the cultivator.

1.2.1 Systems of Agricultural Marketing during British Rule: During the pre-Independence period, Indian agriculture was backward and stagnant and there was hardly any marketable surplus. Therefore, the system of marketing, though defective, did not attract much attention.

Various systems of agricultural marketing existed in India which were exploitative in nature.

A. Sale to Moneylenders: In most cases, farmers sold away their surplus produce to the village moneylenders and traders at a very low price. The moneylenders and traders bought independently or worked as agents of big merchants of the nearby *mandi* (market). This system was closely related to the problem of rural indebtedness. Farmers who were indebted to moneylenders were forced to sell their produce to them. It is understandable that the price paid by the moneylenders was considerably lower than the market price.

The village moneylender advanced loans to farmers for securing production requirements like seeds, and manures and for meeting other needs. These debts some times carried an understanding or an obligation to sell the produce to or through the lender or his nominee. At the time of sale the position of advantage occupied by the village banker got reflected either in a lower price or unfair weights or delayed settlement.

B. Village *Haats*: Another traditional practice was the sale of produce in the *haats* and *shandies*. *Haats* were (and still are) village markets held once or twice a week and served a small cluster of villages. *Shandies* were also village markets held at longer intervals or on special occasions.

C. Sale in *Mandis*: Marketable surplus was also sold through *mandis* located in various small and large towns. As these *mandis* were located in distant places, therefore the farmers had to carry their produce to the nearby *mandi* and sell it to the wholesalers with the help of brokers. These wholesalers sold that farm produce to the mills and factories and to the retailers who, in turn, sold it to the consumers directly in the retail markets.

The benefits of a regulated market were limited. Without changing the marketing structure the number of middlemen and costs could not be reduced. Efforts in this direction were made in some provinces by organising co-operative marketing. The progress of marketing societies, in spite of immense scope, was slow. The entry of a co-operative even as an agent was not generally favoured by the trade.

D. Co-operative Marketing: At some places, marketing societies were formed by farmers to sell the output collectively to take the advantage of collective bargaining for obtaining a better price.

It is noteworthy that Co-operative Planning Committee (Chairman: R.G. Saraiya) was constituted in January 1945 to draw up a plan of co-operative development in the country. The Committee, which submitted its report in November 1945, felt that supply of credit touches only one aspect of the life of the cultivator and the activities of primary co-operative societies should be so extended as to cover the whole of his life. It recommended, *inter alia*, that multi-purpose society should serve as a centre for general economic improvement. Apart from financing crop production, it should act as an agent for sale of produce to the nearest co-operative marketing organization, serve as milk collecting station for the nearest dairy and provision of veterinary services, maintain agriculture machinery to be jointly used by members and encourage subsidiary occupations by its members.

1.2.2 Defects of Agricultural Marketing System: Following were some of the main defects of the agricultural marketing system in India during British rule:

A. Lack of Storage Facility: There was no proper storage or warehousing facilities for farmers in the villages where they could store their agriculture produce. A part of the produce was damaged either by rats or rains due to the absence of proper storage facilities. Thus, the farmers were forced to sell their surplus produce just after the harvest at un-remunerative price.

B. Distress Sale: Most of the Indian farmers were very poor and thus had no capacity to wait for better price of their produce in the absence of proper credit facilities. Farmers often had to go for even distress sale of their output to the village moneylenders-cum-traders at a very poor price. Most of the farmers were indebted to moneylenders.

C. Lack of Transport Facilities: In the absence of proper road transportation facilities in the rural areas, farmers could not reach nearby *mandis* to sell their produce at a fair price. Thus, they preferred to sell their produce at the village markets itself.

D. Unregulated *Mandis*: The conditions of the *mandis* were also not at all favourable to the farmers. In the mandis, the farmers had to wait for disposing their produce for which there was no storage facilities. Thus, the farmers had to lake help of the middleman who took away a major share of the profit, and finalized the deal in favour of the wholesalers. A large number of intermediaries existed between the cultivator and the consumer. All these middlemen claimed a good amount of margin and thus reduced the returns to the cultivators. Dealers in the unregulated markets adopted various malpractices. Prevalence of false weights and measures and lack of grading and standardization of products in these markets were always against the interest of ignorant, small and poor farmers.

E. Lack of Market Intelligence: There was absence of market intelligence or information system. Farmers were not aware of the ruling prices of their produce prevailing in big markets. Thus, they had to accept any un-remunerative price for their produce as offered by traders or middlemen.

F. Lack of Organization: There was lack of collective organization on the part of farmers. A very small amount of marketable surplus was brought to the markets by a huge number of small farmers leading to a high transportation cost. In this context, the Royal Commission on Agriculture in India (1928) had rightly observed, "So long as the farmer does not learn the system of marketing himself or in cooperation with others, he can never bargain better with the buyers of his produce who are very shrewd and well informed".

G. Lack of Grading: Farmers did not give importance to grading of their produce. They hesitated to separate the qualitatively good crops from bad crops. Therefore, they failed to fetch a good price of their quality product.

H. Lack of Institutional Finance: In the absence of adequate institutional finance, farmers had to approach traders and moneylenders for taking loan. After harvest they had to sell their produce to those moneylenders at unfavourable terms.

In short, farmers marketed their product under adverse circumstances. A huge number of small and marginal farmers were forced by the rich farmers, traders and moneylenders to fall into their trap to go for distress sale of their produce by involving them into a vicious circle of indebtedness. All this worsened the income distribution pattern of the village economy of the country.

1.2.3 Role of Co-operatives in Marketing: Co-operatives have an important role to play in input supply, marketing, agro-processing and other agri-businesses to protect farmers from the vagaries of market imperfections.

In India, as in many other countries, co-operation started as a means of ensuring for the poorly equipped citizens advantages which better placed persons were able to command by their own individual resources. The principle of mutual aid, which is the basis of co-operative organisation, and the practice of thrift and self-help which sustain it, generate a sturdy feeling of self-reliance which is of basic importance in a democratic way of life. By pooling their experience and knowledge and by helping one another, members of co-operative societies can not only find the solutions of individual problems but also become better citizens.

In an unregulated economy, the terms of contract are frequently weighted in favour of persons of large means. Those who have the command of scarce resources are left free to drive a bargain with those who need such resources but are ill-equipped to compete for their possession. In a relatively stagnant agricultural economy of small holders, undergoing a transition from barter to money economy and from local to national and international exchange, the possession of capital naturally confers a strategic advantage.

When co-operation was first introduced under the Co-operative Credit Societies Act, 1904, it was confined to the organisation of the co-operative credit societies in urban and rural areas with a view to relieving indebtedness and promoting thrift. The Co-operative Societies Act, 1912, permitted the registration of co-operative societies for promoting non-credit activities as well as federations of primary societies into organisations at higher levels. Both in the field of credit and of non-credit activities the co-operative structure consists of primary societies at the base in villages or towns, central organisations at the district level and apex organisations at the State level.

A large number of consumer stores came into existence for the distribution of controlled commodities during and after the Second World War.

1.2.4 Findings of Royal Commission on Agriculture in India, 1928: Describing the state of marketing of agricultural produce, the Royal Commission on Agriculture in India (1928) remarked, "Markets in India are numerous. In Bihar and Orissa, for instance, there are no less than 432 principal markets and 2,464 minor markets. In all provinces, markets vary greatly in character and importance. At one end of the scale are the elaborate modern mandis of the Punjab canal colonies which consist of a set of shops built round three or four sides of a rectangle, a wide brick pavement being provided for unloading, examining, cleaning, weighing and bagging the grain. In front of the pavement, there is a wide metalled road surrounding an open space used for parking carts. The market is as near to the railway goods platform as possible and sometimes a railway siding runs into it. In such markets, grain is the main product sold. Cotton on the way to the market is frequently intercepted by the agents of the ginneries who also, to an increasing extent, buy it before it leaves the village. Cotton brought into the market is nominally sold there before being carted to the ginneries where the real sale takes place. Adjacent to the grain market are cotton ginneries, a market for imported timber, iron and steel, and bazaars, the shops in which supply everything that the cultivator requires and which is not available in his own village. At the other end of the scale are the small village markets which are often little more than open spaces with accommodation of a very temporary character.

The organisation of the different markets also varies widely. In Bihar and Orissa, all markets are privately owned and rents or tolls are levied by the landholder on whose lands they are situated or by a person who holds a lease from him. In most provinces, there are both public and private markets, the former being directly under the control of a district board or municipality and the latter being licensed by the local authority concerned. It is only in Berar that the constitution of markets is regulated by special legislation, the Berar Cotton and Grain Markets Law of 1897, and that their management is in the hands of elected committees". [1]

1.2.5 Agricultural Produce (Grading and Marketing) Act, 1937: Even though the Royal Commission on Agriculture in India (1928) had recommended the setting up of suitable agencies for development of marketing, provincial governments found it difficult to take action owing to financial stringency. The Government of India, however, was convinced that improved agricultural marketing would facilitate quicker economic recovery. As a first step, an expert was appointed on the staff of the ICAR in April 1934. The office of the Agricultural Marketing Adviser at the Centre and Provincial Marketing Departments came into being in the following year. They jointly conducted marketing surveys for various crops and made recommendations for improving their marketing.

With the enactment of the Agricultural Produce (Grading and Marketing) Act, 1937, progress was also made in grading and standardization of agricultural produce. In the Central Provinces, Agricultural Produce Markets Act was passed for the establishment of regulated markets in commodities other than cotton, particularly rice, wheat and oilseeds.

Among other important developments, mention might be made of the establishment of the Central Jute Committee (1936) for promoting the cultivation and marketing of jute.

In the post-Independence period and particularly after the green revolution, agricultural marketing has become a prime concern for the planners. Due to increase in agricultural productivity, the marketable surplus has increased, necessitating reforms in the existing system. The objectives of these reforms are to ensure: (a) fair prices for the produce of the farmers, (b) adequate and regular availability of foodgrains for urban areas and (c) regular supplies of raw materials for the industries.

1.3 Agricultural Commerce

During the period 1780-1860, India changed from being an exporter of processed goods, for which it received payment in bullion, to being an exporter of raw materials and a buyer of manufactured goods. More specifically, in the 1750s mostly fine cotton and silk were exported from India to markets in Europe, Asia, and Africa. By the second quarter of the 19th century, raw materials, which chiefly consisted of raw cotton, opium, and indigo, accounted for most of India's exports. Also, from the late 18th century British cotton mill industry began to lobby the government to both tax Indian imports and allow them access to markets in India. Starting in the 1830s, British textiles began to appear in the Indian markets.

The American Civil War too had a major impact on India's cotton economy. With the outbreak of the war, American cotton was no longer available to British manufacturers. Resultantly, demand for Indian cotton soared, and the prices soon quadrupled. This led many farmers in India to switch to cultivating cotton as a quick cash crop. However, with the end of the war in 1865, the demand plummeted again, creating another downturn in the agricultural economy.

1.3.1 Cotton and Textiles: Cotton stood easily first in the list of Indian exports of raw produce. In spite of the work of the Indian Central Cotton Committee, and of the joint action by cotton trade associations which the Indian Central Cotton Committee was endeavouring to secure, adulteration prevailed to an undesirable degree. These malpractices were checked by the operation of the Cotton Ginning and Pressing Factories Act of 1925, under the provisions of which mixed, adulterated or damped cotton could be traced back not only to the factory which ginned it but also to the original owner. The prevalence of the practice of mixing short with long staple cotton seriously hampered the work of the agricultural departments in spreading improved varieties.

Cotton and silk goods of India could be sold for a profit in the British market at a price significantly lower than those fabricated in Britain. It consequently became necessary to protect the latter by duties or by positive prohibition. Had this not been the case, the mills of Manchester would have been closed. They were created by the sacrifice of the Indian manufactures. Had India been an independent country, it would have retaliated by imposing preventive duties on British goods. This act of self-defence was not permitted because India was at the mercy of colonial rulers. British goods were forced upon India without paying any duty.

Cotton's rise to global importance came about as a result of the cultural transformation of Europe and Britain's trading empire. Calico and chintz, types of cotton fabrics, became popular in Europe, and by 1664 the East India Company was importing a quarter of a million pieces into Britain. By the 18th century, the middle class had become more concerned with cleanliness and fashion, and there was a demand for easily washable and colourful fabric. Wool continued to dominate the European markets, but cotton prints were introduced to Britain by the East India Company in the 1690s. Imports of calicoes, cheap cotton fabrics from Kozhikode, then known as *Calicut*, in India, found a mass market among the poor. By 1721, these calicoes threatened British manufacturers, and Parliament passed the Calico Act that banned calicoes for clothing or domestic purposes. In 1774, the Act was repealed with the invention of machines that allowed for British manufacturers to compete with Eastern fabrics.

Indian cotton textiles, particularly those from Bengal, continued to maintain a competitive advantage up until the 19th century. In order to compete with India, Britain invested in labour-saving technology, while implementing protectionist policies such as bans and tariffs to restrict Indian imports. At the same time, the East India Company's rule in India opened up a new market for British goods, while the capital amassed from Bengal after its 1757 conquest was used to invest in British industries such as textile manufacturing and greatly increase British wealth.

British colonization also forced open the large Indian market to British goods, which could be sold in India without tariffs or duties, compared to local Indian producers, while raw cotton was imported from India without tariffs to British factories which manufactured textiles from Indian cotton, giving Britain a monopoly over India's large market and cotton resources. India served as both a significant supplier of raw goods to British manufacturers and a large captive market for British manufactured goods. Britain eventually surpassed India as the world's leading cotton textile manufacturer in the 19th century.

The cotton industry grew under the British commercial empire. British cotton products were successful in European markets, constituting 40.5 percent of exports in 1784-1786. Britain's success was also due to its trade with its own colonies, whose settlers maintained British identities, and thus, fashions. With the growth of the cotton industry, manufacturers had to find new sources of raw cotton, and cultivation was expanded to West India.

High tariffs against Indian textile workshops, British power in India through the East India Company, and British restrictions on Indian cotton imports transformed India from the source of textiles to a source of raw cotton. Cultivation was also attempted in the Caribbean and West Africa, but these attempts failed due to bad weather and poor soil. The Indian sub-continent was looked to as a possible source of raw cotton, but intra-imperial conflicts and economic rivalries prevented the area from producing the necessary supply.

1.3.2 Jute and Jute Manufactures: The jute trade was centred mainly in India, particularly in the province of Bengal. Due to its natural fertile soil, Bengal jute was exported to South East Asia from the 17th century by the Dutch, French and later by other Europeans. By the 1790s a small export had developed to the Scottish city of Dundee, where the flax spinning industry could use a small percentage to lower costs. Thomas Neigh, a Dundee merchant invented the mechanical process of spinning jute in 1833 by first soaking it in whale oil.

Raw jute was exported from Bengal by British merchants in increasing quantities from the 1840s replacing flax in the Dundee mills. The mill owners creatively developed new markets for the jute goods, principally sacks, worldwide.

In 1858, Indian financiers supported the importation of spinning machinery from Dundee in order to create their own industry. The Indian jute barons were able to pay workers less and gradually began to take over. By 1895, jute industries in Bengal overtook the Scottish jute trade. Many Scots worked in Bengal to set up jute factories for Indians, dominated by Marwari brokers. Jute coffee bags are perhaps the most famous product, known as hessian. They found a military use starting in the Crimean War. In First World War, the government awarded the entire contract for sandbags to a Greek-Indian firm in Calcutta.

The British East India Company was the British Empire Authority delegated in Bengal from the 17th century until dissolved in 1857. The Dutch and the French were the first jute traders. By 1908 Calcutta was the world's largest jute producer having defeated Dundee. From the 1890s the Marwaris had entered the market as brokers (like the Birla group) and became the dominant owners of an industry employing over 3,00,000 workers.

1.3.3 Wheat and Barley: Wheat and barley occupied an important position in India's exports to Britain and other countries. The Royal Commission on Agriculture (1928) noted, "Wheat was most excellently packed and graded, that it was almost the only grain which is always sold on the basis of analysis for impurity, that its quality is usually very even and that the allowances which have to be paid by the seller to the buyer for inferiority of quality are usually of minor importance...Bags in which Indian grain is packed are usually better than any other bags used in the grain trade and that the stowage in ships is an example of excellence...Most of the Indian wheat imported into Great Britain attracts millers in that country partly by reason of its extreme dryness, and partly owing to the fact that its presence in flour promotes the rapid growth of yeast...The bulk of Indian wheat exported to Great Britain reaches that country in the months of June, July and August, at which season of the year it fills a gap in the supplies of "soft" wheat imported from other countries...We have considered the possibilities of the export of high-grade Indian wheat in volume and regularity sufficient to create and sustain a definite demand. We think that, from the agricultural point of view, no insuperable difficulties prevent the production of a strong wheat capable of entering overseas markets on a plane of quality and of average price well above that at present enjoyed by Indian wheat. It has been established that many of the improved varieties of Indian wheat yield flour and loaves of the same class as strong American wheat, and that strong, free-milling wheat can be grown in India". [2]

1.3.4 Opium: Opium was for the large part of the 19th Century, the second-most important source of revenue for the colonial state. It was only out-matched by land taxes.

The government's opium industry was one of the largest enterprises on the sub-continent, producing a few thousand tons of the drug every year. More importantly, the crop had a lasting negative impact on the lives of millions.

Interest-free advance payments were offered to poppy farmers who could not access easy credit. By itself, this was not a bad thing for those producing for the global market. What made it bad for them was that what they paid for rent, manure, irrigation and hired workers was higher than the income from the sale of raw opium. In other words, the price peasants received for their opium did not even cover the cost of growing it. Moreover, they were soon trapped in a web of contractual obligations from which it was difficult to escape.

Stiff production targets fixed by the opium agencies also meant that farmers could not decide whether or not to produce opium. They were forced to submit part of their land and labour to the colonial government's export strategy.

Local landowners forced their landless tenants to grow poppy. The peasants were also kidnapped, arrested and threatened with destruction of crops, criminal prosecution and jail if they refused to grow the crop. It was a highly coercive system.

At this time, the East India Company's trade with China began to grow as well. In the early 19th century demand for Chinese tea had greatly increased in Britain. Since the money supply in India was restricted and the Company was indisposed to shipping bullion from Britain, it decided upon opium, which had a large underground market in China and which was grown in many parts of India, as the most profitable form of payment. However, since the Chinese authorities had banned the importation and consumption of opium, the Company engaged them in the First Opium War, and at its conclusion, under the Treaty of Nanjing, gained access to five Chinese ports, Guangzhou, Xiamen, Fuzhou, Shanghai, and Ningbo. In addition, Hong Kong was ceded to the British Crown. Towards the end of the second quarter of the 19th century, opium export constituted 40 percent of India's exports.

By 1915, the opium trade with China, the biggest market, had ended. However, the British Indian monopoly on opium continued until India won Independence in 1947.

1.3.5 Indigo: Another major export item was indigo [3] dye, which was extracted from natural indigo, and which came to be grown in Bengal and northern Bihar. Bengal was the world's largest producer of natural indigo in the 19th century. In late 17th and early 18th century Europe, blue apparel was favoured as a fashion, and blue uniforms were common in the military. Hence, the demand for the dye was high. In 1788, the East India Company offered advances to ten British planters to grow indigo. However, since the property rights defined in the Permanent Settlement did not allow Europeans to buy agricultural land, they had to, in turn, offer cash advances to local peasants, and sometimes coerce them to grow the crop. The European demand for the dye, however, proved to be unstable, and both creditors and cultivators bore the risk of the market crashes in 1827 and 1847. The peasant discontent in Bengal eventually led to the *Indigo rebellion* in 1859-60 and to the end of indigo production there. [4] In Bihar, however, indigo production continued well into the 20th century. The centre of indigo production there, Champaran district, became the staging ground, in 1917, for Mahatma Gandhi's first experiment in non-violent resistance against the British Raj.

Indigo industry was fostered and developed by the servants of East India Company, and attained the zenith of its prosperity under the management and care of British capitalists, planters and traders. Many of the planters attained great wealth, owned large estates, and settled down to live the lives of country gentlemen in the tropics. For nearly a century, they had almost monopoly of the production of one of the most valuable and essential dyes known to commerce.

Endnotes

1. *Report of the Royal Commission on Agriculture in India, 1928*, pp. 382-385.
2. *Ibid.,* pp. 399-400.
3. Indigo is a plant that is used to create dyes for many different purposes, such as to dye clothing, dyes for ink, and dyes as a

paint. Indigo has been around the world in different places for thousands of years, but the one primary indigo species that is used is from India.

4. The Indigo revolt was a peasant movement and subsequent uprising of indigo farmers against the indigo planters that arose in Chaugacha village of Nadia in Bengal in 1859.

2

Indian Agriculture at a Glance

Achievement of rapid and sustainable growth in any country is critically dependent on its ability to use and manage its natural resources effectively. The most important natural resource of any country is land which is the base for agricultural production.

2.1 Why is Agriculture Important for Less Developed Countries (LDCs)?

In looking back on the history of the present day developed countries, one can see that agriculture played an important part in the process of their enrichment. For one thing, if development is to occur, agriculture must be able to produce a surplus of food to maintain the growing non-agricultural labour force. Since food is more essential for life than are the services provided by merchants or bankers or insurers, an economy cannot shift to such activities unless food is available for barter or sale in sufficient quantities to support those engaged in them. Unless food can be obtained through international trade, a country does not normally develop industrially until its farm areas can supply its towns with food in exchange for the products of their factories.

Economic development also requires a growing labour force. In an agricultural country most of the workers needed must come from the rural population. Thus, agriculture must not only supply a surplus of food for the towns, but it must also be able to produce the increased amount of food with a relatively smaller labour force. It may do so by substituting animal power for human power or by gradually introducing labour-saving machinery. Agriculture may also be a source of the capital needed for industrial development to the extent that it provides a surplus that may be converted into the funds needed to purchase industrial equipment or to build roads and provide public services.

For these reasons, a country seeking to develop its economy may well be advised to give a significant priority to agriculture. Experience in the developing countries has shown that agriculture can be made much more productive with the proper investment in irrigation systems, research, fertilizers, insecticides, and herbicides.

Fortunately, many advances in applied science do not require massive amounts of capital, although it may be necessary to expand marketing and transportation facilities so that farm output can be brought to the entire population.

One difficulty in giving priority to agriculture is that most of the increase in farm output and most of the income gains are concentrated in certain regions rather than extending throughout the country. The remaining farmers are not able to produce more and actually suffer a disadvantage as farm prices decline. There is no easy answer to that problem, but developing countries need to be aware of it.

As economic development proceeds, a large proportion of the farm labour force must shift from agriculture into other pursuits. That fundamental shift in the labour force is made possible, of course, by an enormous increase in output per worker as agriculture becomes modernized. That increase in output stems from various factors. Where land is plentiful, the output per worker is likely to be higher because it is possible to employ more fertilizer and machinery per worker.

Land is a fixed resource. There is a conflict regarding the allocation of available land between agriculture, industry and urban use. It is important to recognise that diversion of land from agricultural to non-agricultural uses is inevitable in any development process since industry must expand and so also cities and in both cases land needed can only come from agriculture. Concern is often raised in this context about the impact on food security. This problem is greatly exaggerated because the productivity of land in agriculture in less developed countries (LDCs) at present is very low and the shift of some land from agriculture to non-agricultural use can easily be offset by productivity increases, which are feasible and have been seen in many other developed countries.

A strong agricultural economy brings social progress by increasing productivity, employment and income. Agriculture is the main driver of development in most rural areas. Demand for staple foods, agricultural commodities and processed food is growing in developing countries. To meet these needs, the agricultural and food sectors must be modernized.

2.2 Role of Agriculture in the Indian Economy

The largest portion of the natural resources of India consists of land and by far the largest number of its inhabitants is engaged in agriculture. Therefore, in any scheme of economic development of the country, agriculture holds a position of basic importance.

Although Indian agriculture is way back compared to the levels in developed countries, some notable developments have occurred over the post-Independence period. Large areas which suffered from repeated failures of rainfall have received irrigation, new crops have come to occupy a significant position in the country's production and trade, agricultural and the industrial economies in the country now exert a powerful influence on one another, problems of rural indebtedness and the exploitative practices of the village moneylenders are much less, and finally there is already in the countryside an awakening and a desire for improved standard of living.

Agriculture being a state subject, the primary responsibility for increasing agriculture production, enhancing productivity, and exploring the vast untapped potential of the sector rests with the State Governments. However, in order to supplement the efforts of the State Governments, a number of Centrally-sponsored and Central Sector schemes are being implemented for enhancing agricultural production and productivity in the country and increasing the income of the farming community.

Agricultural sector occupies a key position in the Indian economy. Agriculture (inclusive of animal husbandry, forestry and fishing) is central to the nutrition needs of India and also remains the largest sector of India's economy as a source of employment.

According to the Annual Report of the Ministry of Agriculture and Farmers' Welfare, 2020-21, "Agriculture plays a vital role in India's economy. 54.6 percent of the total workforce is engaged in agriculture and allied sector activities (Census 2011) and accounts for 17.8 percent of the country's gross value added (GVA) for the year 2019-20 (at current prices)". [1]

The First Five Year Plan (1951-52 to 1955-56) accorded the highest priority to the agricultural sector to tide over the difficult food problem created by the partition of the country. Agriculture has occupied an important place in every successive plan. Two major components of agricultural development strategy have been: (a) subsidies on inputs and (b) minimum support price for output.

Agricultural products like cereals (mainly rice), tea, coffee, cashew, spices, tobacco and leather are important items of India's exports and hence foreign exchange earnings.

There is inter-dependence between agriculture and industry. The development of the agricultural sector depends, to a large extent, on such core industries as power, petroleum, fertilisers, insecticides and agricultural machinery (tractors, harvesters and pump sets). Industry, on the other hand, depends on agriculture for the supply of raw material for agro-based industries including textiles, cigarettes, jute, sugar, paper, processed foodstuffs and *vanaspati*.

2.3 Components of Agriculture and Allied Sectors

India is the land of diverse agro-ecologies. It produces a number of major and minor agricultural commodities.

There are two main agricultural seasons in India: (a) *kharif* under which crops are planted at the onset of the Southwest monsoon in June-July and harvested in September-October, and (b) *rabi* under which crops are planted usually between October and December and harvested between March and May. Major *kharif* crops are rice, jowar, bajra, maize, cotton, sugarcane, soyabean and groundnut. Major *rabi* crops are wheat, barley, gram, linseed, rapeseed and mustard.

Due to its diverse climatic, soil and terrain conditions, a wide variety of crops are grown in different parts of the country. The cropping pattern in India is influenced by a host of factors. Cropping pattern refers to the distribution of cultivated land among different crops grown in a country. Cropping pattern reveals the nature of agricultural operations, e.g. the importance of food crops vis-à-vis cash crops. Cropping pattern is influenced by a host of factors which can be broadly classified into two categories: (a) physical factors and (b) economic factors.

There has been no significant change in the cropping pattern during the post-Independence period. The present cropping pattern is unbalanced as it is heavily tilted in favour of paddy and wheat while area under oilseeds and pulses is less than required.

Among the physical factors, the important ones are soil conditions, extent of rainfall and type of climate. The economic factors include relative prices of agricultural commodities, size of the farms, availability of inputs, demand conditions, system of land holding and government policy regarding exports, imports, taxes and subsidies.

Agriculture and allied sectors in India consist of the following 4 sub-sectors: (a) crop sector, (b) livestock, (c) fisheries and (d) forestry.

2.3.1 Crop Sector: Being the largest sector in agriculture, crop sector holds a large number of contributors, viz. field crops, plantation crops and horticultural crops. This sector constitutes the backbone of the India's food economy.

A. Field Crops: These include the following:

1. Cereals (paddy, wheat, barley, maize, gram and other cereals).
2. Pulses (gram, blackgram, moth, other pulses).
3. Oilseeds (linseed, sesame, groundnut, mustard, soyabean, sunflower, rapeseed).
4. Fibres (cotton, jute, mesta and others).
5. Sugarcane.

B. Plantation Crops: These include the following:

1. Tea, coffee, tobacco, opium, betel leaves, saffron, cocoa, rubber, coconut, cashew.
2. Condiments and spices (cardamom, chillies, black pepper, turmeric, cumin, fenugreek, tamarind, cloves, nutmeg). Some of these crops constitute important items of India's exports. India is the largest producer, processor, consumer and exporter of cashew in the world. Coconut is an important tree crop grown extensively in coastal areas providing livelihood to about 10 million people in cultivation, processing and related activities.

C. Horticultural Crops: These consist of the following:

1. Fruits (banana, mango, grapes, papaya, apple, orange and others).
2. Vegetables (potato, onion, tomato, radish, carrot, green peas, and others).

2.3.2 Livestock: It consists of the following: (a) milk, meat, eggs, (b) wool and hair, (c) silkworm and honey cocoon and (d) dung.

2.3.3 Fisheries: It comprises: (a) inland fish and (b) marine fish.

2.3.4 Forestry: This sector is composed of: (a) industrial wood, (b) firewood and (c) non-timber forest products.

2.4 Subsistence Nature of Farming and Small-sized Holdings

As against the commercialised nature of agricultural operations in the developed countries, farming in India still remains a source of livelihood for most farmers in India. The main reason for this is the low per capita availability of land.

The average size of farms has become smaller over the years and the trend continues. An important reason for this trend is the growth of population which has adversely affected the per capita availability of land. The pressure of population along with some social and economic factors has decreased the size of agricultural holdings in India. Various surveys conducted by official agencies point out this fact. Moreover, traditional agricultural practices still prevail in large parts of the country. Use of modern agricultural technology has remained confined to few pockets of affluent farmers in select States.

In the above context, the Twelfth Five Year Plan (2012-13 to 2016-17) observed, "Although half of India's population continues to depend on agriculture as its primary source of livelihood, 83 percent of farmers operate holdings of less than 2 hectare in size, and the average holding size is only 1.23 hectare. This is often in fragments and unirrigated. There are also those who are entirely landless, although agriculture is their main source of livelihood. They have inadequate financial resources to purchase and often depend on leasing in small plots, on insecure terms, for short periods, sometimes only for one season. Hence many face insecurity of tenure and the growing threat of land alienation and pressures from urbanisation, industrialisation and powerful interests.

They are unable to take advantage of the economies of scale, or invest in lumpy inputs such as irrigation, technology or machinery. They have limited access to formal credit. Hence, they have few resources for land improvement or crop insurance or adequate inputs (seeds, fertilisers, and so on). They are often ignored by extension agencies and seldom receive information on new technologies or training in skill-intensive agricultural practices". [2]

2.4.1 Reasons for Small Holdings: There are various reasons for sub-division and fragmentation of holdings in India.

1. The laws of inheritance in India give to all children an equal share in the property of their parents. After the enactment of the Hindu Succession Act, 1956, daughters have also become, along with sons, entitled to an equal share in the property of their parents. Consequently, land is being sub-divided with every passing generation.
2. As already noted, the population of India has increased rapidly after Independence. It increased from 36.1 crore in 1951 to 43.9 crore in 1961, to 54.8 crore in 1971 and to 68.5 crore in 1981. The census of 1991 enumerated the population at 84.4 crore which increased to 100.6 crore in 2001 and was enumerated at 121 crore in the 2011 Census. However, the area of agricultural land has remained almost the same. Moreover, due to lack of employment opportunities in the non-agricultural sector, most of the additional labour force has to fall back on agriculture for earning a living.
3. Decline of joint family system has also contributed to the break up of agricultural holdings. Legal heirs prefer to have their individual shares in family property instead of holding it as joint property of the family. The rise of individualism in modern societies has hastened the decline of joint family system.
4. Rural indebtedness has also contributed to the sub-division and fragmentation of holdings. As is well-known, most farmers in India are indebted to moneylenders and landlords. In the event of non-payment of their debt, they are forced to sell a portion of their land to the creditor.
5. It is a common practice in India to lease out land to tenants on crop-sharing basis. Quite often the landlords lease out their land to a number of tenants to avoid trouble and also to circumvent the land laws. Due to these practices, land gets sub-divided and fragmented.

2.4.2 Disadvantages of Small Holdings: Sub-division of holdings leads to loss of cultivable land due to boundaries. Too many boundaries cause disputes, often leading to litigation. Instead of investing their precious resources in improving the productivity of land, farmers waste their limited funds in settling claims and counter claims. This tendency has created tensions in rural areas.

Fragmented holdings create difficulties in the management of land resources. When a farmer has to shift from one piece of land to another, it involves wastage of manpower and extra expenses. Similarly, small-sized farms restrict opportunities for the use of modern science and technology. Proper arrangements for irrigation cannot be made if farms belonging to a farmer are scattered here and there. Modern agricultural machines cannot be successfully operated on tiny farms. Absence or limited use of modern agricultural practices keeps farm productivity low.

In this context, a NITI Aayog document remarked, "Over the years, landholdings in India have become smaller and fragmented. According to the 2010-11 Agricultural Census, 47 percent of landholdings had become less than half a hectare in size. These holdings are too small to support a family of five so that many farmers now seek alternative sources of income. But stringent tenancy laws in most states have meant that these farmers hesitate to lease the land they leave behind. As a result, an increasing amount of farmland is being left fallow. The introduction of a modern land-leasing law that balances and protects the rights of the tenant and landowners would be a potential solution". [3]

2.4.3 Farm Size and Productivity: What is the ideal size of a holding? The ideal size of a holding (called economic holding or optimum holding) is one which allows the most efficient use of land, labour and capital with a given technique of production. It is difficult to prescribe a uniform size of economic holding for all crops and for all regions. In fact, the size of economic holding depends upon a host of factors such as nature of the crop, fertility of soil and technique of production.

There is a great debate among agricultural economists in India regarding the relationship between size of farms and productivity/profitability. Productivity simply means output per hectare of land while farm-profitability relates to the value of output over all costs of cultivation. Some experts have argued that as farm size increases, productivity also increases. However, some researchers hold the opposite view and maintain that productivity declines as farm size increases.

Although the debate is inconclusive and the picture confusing, it has been reasonably well established by statistical studies that farm size and productivity are inversely related. The myth that small farms are inefficient has been exploded. The opponents of land ceiling laws always criticised the break up of large farms on efficiency ground. Since the efficiency of small farms has nearly been confirmed, the case for land ceiling on equity ground has become stronger.

2.5 Low Productivity of Indian Agriculture

Indian agriculture was backward and stagnant at the time of Independence. Ever since the launching of the First Five Year Plan (1951-56), agricultural sector has received the prime attention of the Government in the overall strategy of economic development. As a result, farm productivity has increased over the years and the country has achieved high degree of self-sufficiency in terms of foodgrains and raw material for agro-based industries (Table 2.1). Although per hectare yield of major crops has increased over the years yet it is far below the international levels. This scenario calls for an examination of the causes of low productivity of agriculture in India.

Table 2.1: Trends in the Productivity of Indian Agriculture: Selected Years

(yield per hectare/kg.)

Crop	1980-81	1990-91	2000-01	2010-11	2020-21
Rice	1,336	1,740	1,901	2,239	2,713
Wheat	1,630	2,281	2,708	2,988	3,464
Coarse cereals	695	900	1,027	1,531	2,146
Pulses	473	578	544	691	892

Source: Reserve Bank of India, *Handbook of Statistics on Indian Economy*, September 15, 2021, Table 21 (excerpted).

2.5.1 Causes of Low Productivity: Statistical evidence suggests that farm productivity in India is low as compared to other countries of the world. The low productivity of the agricultural sector is attributable to a host of technological and institutional factors. Some of the important of these factors are described below.

A. Technological Factors: These include the following.

1. **Lack of Irrigation Facilities:** Despite best efforts during the last five decades, only one-third of cultivated land has the facility of artificial irrigation. In other words, most of the farmers depend on uncertain rainfall for irrigation of their fields. Rainfall is uncertain in terms of quantity, place and time. Agriculture is still a gamble in monsoon for millions of farmers in this country.
2. **Limited Use of Fertilisers:** Adequate use of fertilisers is crucial for improving the farm productivity. Unfortunately, the use of fertilisers by Indian farmers is much below the level achieved in developed countries.
3. **Limited Use of High Yield Variety of Seeds:** The HYV programme was started in 1966. The percentage of HYV area to total area differs from crop to crop. In the case of wheat it is quite high. However, the coverage of area under HYV for other crops is relatively low.
4. **Inadequate Plant Protection Schemes:** Another reason for low productivity is the damage caused to crops by insects, pests, and plant diseases. The use of pesticides and insecticides is not widespread, particularly among the small and marginal farmers. Central Integrated Pest Management Centres have been set up in various States to monitor crop pests, and to organise training in pest management for extension workers and farmers.
5. **Lack of Farm Mechanisation:** Most Indian farmers still use age-old farming techniques like wooden plough, cattle power, and sickle. The use of modern farm machinery is limited to affluent farmers in selected regions of the country. There is a great deal of controversy regarding

mechanisation of agriculture in view of widespread unemployment and disguised unemployment in rural areas. Therefore, the policy regarding mechanisation of agriculture has to be cautious and selective.

6. **Floods and Soil Erosion:** Floods are a common occurrence in one or the other part of the country every year. The consequent soil erosion and waterlogging dislocates production cycle, resulting in loss of agricultural output.
7. **Lack of Agricultural Research:** Agricultural research is of a continuing nature. New knowledge has to be gained, and fresh problems tackled. The role of universities in promoting agricultural research is a question which needs attention. Although universities are eminently suited for such research, especially of the more fundamental type, they have not taken it up to any significant extent in the past, owing perhaps to lack of funds and other causes. Limitations in the way of the universities to take an appropriate part in agricultural research should be removed and the universities encouraged to make their contribution to research. This will benefit the universities also by bringing their scientific staffs into direct contact with real problems which are in urgent need of solution for the betterment of the vast majority of rural people. Extension is another element needing urgent attention alongside research. New methods and approaches need to be devised for agricultural extension using information technology and mobile technology. Local participation of progressive farmers, self-help groups and agricultural co-operative societies should be leveraged to help transfer technology through one-to-one exchange of information.

B. Institutional Factors: Use of modern methods of production is conditioned by the institutional framework of a production sector. If the institutional set up is exploitative, it will discourage the adoption of efficient technology. Unfortunately, the institutional setting of the farm sector in India is not congenial for the use of modern agricultural technology.

1. **Feudal Land Relations:** Although *zamindari* system was abolished soon after Independence, it continues to exist in a different garb. Land reform laws have proved ineffective and therefore big landlords still rule the roost in rural areas. They lease out their land to tenants and charge high rents. The various tenancy malpractices hardly provide any incentive to tenant farmers to improve land and productivity.
2. **Small-sized Holdings:** As a result of population growth, there is tremendous pressure on available cultivable land. This has led to overcrowding and hence sub-division and fragmentation of holdings. Small-sized and scattered holdings imply wastage of time and labour, difficulties in the use of modern techniques, and quarrels and litigation among farmers. The existence of these problems is also responsible for poor farm yield.
3. **Rural Indebtedness:** Poverty of the Indian farmer forces him to borrow money for his existence. The institution of money lending is the greatest curse for the poor and illiterate rural folk of India. Although the importance of moneylenders has declined over the last 55 years, they are still very dominant in providing credit to the farmers. The exploitative practices of the moneylenders are no secret. Their malpractices include charging of high rate of interest and adopting unfair means in the maintenance of accounts.
4. **Marketing Difficulties:** Marketing is the last ring in the production chain. If the marketing system is inefficient and denies the farmers a reasonable return for their efforts, they will be discouraged to produce more. Unfortunately, the present marketing system of agricultural produce is not favourable to the interests of the farmers. The preponderance of intermediaries and the malpractices of commission agents deny remunerative prices to the farmers.

Thus, low productivity in Indian agriculture is the result of a number of technological and institutional factors which influence each other. The causes of low agricultural productivity explained above suggest their own remedies.

The central challenge of Indian agriculture is low productivity, evident in modest average yields, especially in pulses. India happens to be the major producer and consumer of pulses, which is one of the major sources of protein for the population. India has low yields comparable to most countries. Imports cannot be the main source for meeting domestic demand for pulses. Therefore, policy must incentivise movement of resources towards production of pulses.

The production pattern for pulses is very different from other crops. Not only is most of the land dedicated to growing pulses in each state unirrigated, but the national output of pulses comes predominantly from un-irrigated land. In contrast, a large share of output in wheat, rice and sugarcane—in Punjab, Haryana and U.P.—is from irrigated land. In water scarce Maharashtra, all sugarcane is grown on irrigated land. Meeting the high and growing demand for pulses in the country will require large increases in pulses production on irrigated land, but this will not occur if agriculture policies continue to focus largely on cereals and sugarcane.

The negative consequences of low agriculture yields extend from precarious incomes of farmers to large tracts of land locked in low value agriculture, despite growing demands for high value products such as fruits, vegetables, livestock products because of consumption diversification with rising incomes and urbanization.

2.6 Covid-19 and Agricultural Sector

When countrywide lockdown was announced from March 25, 2020, most of the economic activities came to a grinding halt in urban areas. However, rural India continued to be normal in view of the exemption from restrictions allowed to farmers to conduct farming operations, including harvesting and transporting their produce to grain markets with the general conditions of face covering, hand hygiene and social distancing. These exemptions helped to maintain continuity in supply chain, especially in view of harvesting and sowing season. Food Corporation of India and State Governments carried out massive procurement of *rabi* crops, mainly wheat.

Not only cultivation, but agriculture-related activities—plantation, horticulture, cattle breeding, fishing, poultry farming, dairy farming—also remained, by and large, immune to Covid crisis and their future growth is assured.

India's foodgrains production was 285 million tonnes (MT) in 2018-19 which rose to record level of 295 MT in 2019-20. The target for 2021-22 was set at 316 MT.

2.6.1 Aatmanirbar Bharat and Agricultural Sector: Prime Minister Narendra Modi announced on May 12, 2020, the Aatmanirbhar Bharat Abhiyan which combined relief, policy reforms and fiscal and monetary measures to help businesses and individuals to cope with the situation created by Covid-19 pandemic. A mega package of ₹ 20 lakh crore (10 percent of GDP) was announced for the purpose.

The details of the ₹ 20 lakh crore package were announced by Finance Minister Nirmala Sitharaman in five tranches during the next five consecutive days. All the measures were aimed at spurring investment and buffering the economy against the Covid pandemic shock. The third tranche, announced on May 15, 2020, pertained to a mix of financial, legislative and other reform measures aimed largely at increasing the pricing power of farmers.

The sector has got renewed thrust due to various measures on credit, market reforms and food processing under the Aatmanirbhar Bharat announcements. Various interventions of the government for the development of allied sectors including animal husbandry, dairying and fisheries exhibit its resolve towards tapping the potential of allied sectors to further enhance farm welfare.

It may be recalled that soon after Independence in 1947 and partition of the country, India suffered heavy deficits in the availability of foodgrains. In 1950-51, total fodgrains production was 50 million tonnes. Over the last 75 years, it has increased almost six-fold. Population has increased around three and a half-fold: from 36 crore in 1951 to 130 crore presently. Thus, the per capita availability of foodgrains has substantially improved and the country is well-placed in terms of basic necessity.

Endnotes

1. Government of India, Ministry of Agriculture and Farmers' Welfare, Department of Agriculture, Co-operation and Farmers' Welfare, *Annual Report 2020-21*, p. 1.
2. Government of India, Planning Commission, *Twelfth Five Year Plan* (2012-17), Volume I, Chapter 6, paras 6.6 and 6.7.
3. NITI Aayog, *India: Three Year Action Agenda (2017-18 to 2019-20)*, August 2017, p. 2.

Part II
Agricultural Finance

3

Credit Needs and Sources of Indian Farmers

Agricultural production in India depends upon millions of small farmers. It is the intensity of their effort and the efficiency of their technique that will help in raising yields per acre. Because of inadequate financial resources and absence of timely credit facilities at reasonable rates, many of the farmers, even though otherwise willing, are unable to go in for improved seeds and manures or to introduce better methods or techniques. It is, therefore, of the utmost importance that the financial requirements of the farmers are adequately met.

3.1 Credit and Agricultural Development

Being the backbone of the Indian economy, agriculture has all along been treated as a priority sector for the allocation of institutional credit. The low growth rate of agriculture in the past few years has further strengthened the channels of credit flow to this sector. Provision of sufficient and timely credit at fair rates of interest has, therefore, to be considered as an integral part of agricultural development. Assistance rendered by way of credit has, however, to be related to specific items of productive work or of essential costs of cultivation. Following guidelines from the RBI, commercial banks are increasingly devoting attention to agricultural sector to meet its credit needs.

Agricultural growth is crucial for alleviating rural poverty. Access to institutional credit to more farmers and appropriate quantity and quality of agricultural credit are crucial for realising the full potential of agriculture as a profitable activity. The government has taken many policy initiatives for strengthening farm credit delivery system for providing credit at affordable rates of interest to support the resource requirements of the agricultural sector. The emphasis of these initiatives has been on providing timely and adequate credit support to farmers with particular focus on small and marginal farmers and weaker sections of society to enable them to adopt modern technology and improved agricultural practices for increasing agricultural production and productivity. The policy essentially lays emphasis on augmenting credit flow at the ground level through credit planning, adoption of region specific strategies and rationalization of lending policies and procedures and bringing down the rate of interest on farm loan.

3.2 Credit Needs of the Indian Farmers

Need for agricultural credit arises because modern farm technology is costly and the personal resources of the farmers are inadequate. Provision of agricultural credit, as an input, is essential for widespread use of improved agricultural methods.

Credit requirements of the farmers may be classified: (a) on the basis of purpose, and (b) on the basis of time. They need credit for productive as well as for unproductive purposes. Productive purposes include all such activities which help in the improvement of agricultural productivity such as purchase of inputs and permanent improvements in land. Unproductive credit needs include celebration of marriages and other social and religious functions and litigation.

Finance required for productive purposes can be divided broadly into the following categories:

1. Short-term (for periods up to 15 months).
2. Medium-term (from 15 months up to 5 years).
3. Long-term (above 5 years).

Short-term loans are required for purchasing seeds, manures and fertilizers or for meeting labour charges etc. These are expected to be repaid after the harvest.

Medium-term loans are granted for purposes such as sinking of wells, purchase of bullocks, pumping plants and other improved implements etc.

Loans repayable over a longer period (i.e. above 5 years) are classified as long-term loans. These are utilised for payment of old debts, purchase of the heavier machines, making permanent improvements and increasing the size of the holding.

3.3 Sources of Credit for the Farmers

Sources of micro credit for the poor are grouped into two categories: (a) institutional sources and (b) non-institutional sources. Institutional sources include co-operative societies, commercial banks and other government agencies. Non-institutional sources comprise moneylenders, landlords, relatives etc.

3.3.1 Institutional (or Formal) Sources: These are as under:

A. Member-owned Organizations: These include self-help groups, credit unions, and a variety of hybrid organizations like financial service associations. Like their informal cousins, they are generally small and local, which means they have access to good knowledge about each other's financial circumstances and can offer convenience and flexibility. Since they are managed by poor people, their costs of operation are low. However, these providers may have little financial skill and can run into trouble when the economy turns down or their operations become too complex. Unless they are effectively regulated and supervised, they can be *captured* by one or two influential leaders, and the members can lose their money.

B. Non-governmental Organizations (NGOs): NGOs have spread around the developing world in the recent past. They have proven very innovative, pioneering banking techniques like solidarity lending, village banking and mobile banking that have overcome barriers to serving poor populations. However, with boards that do not necessarily represent either their capital or their customers, their governance structures can be fragile, and they can become overly dependent on external donors.

C. Formal Financial Institutions: In addition to commercial banks, these include state banks, agricultural development banks, savings banks, rural banks and non-bank financial institutions. They are regulated and supervised, offer a wider range of financial services, and control a branch network that can extend across the country. However, they have proved reluctant to adopt social missions, and due to their high costs of operation, often cannot deliver services to poor or remote populations.

In India, agricultural credit is disbursed through a multi-agency network comprising of commercial banks, regional rural banks and co-operatives. With their vast network (covering almost all the villages in the country), wider coverage and outreach extending to the remotest part of country, the co-operative credit institutions, both in short and long-term structure are the main institutional mechanism for dispensation of agricultural credit.

Agricultural growth is crucial for alleviating rural poverty. Access to institutional credit to more farmers and appropriate quantity and quality of agricultural credit are crucial for realising the full potential of agriculture as a profitable activity.

Provision of sufficient and timely credit at fair rates of interest has, therefore, to be considered as an integral part of agricultural development. Assistance rendered by way of credit has, however, to be related to specific items of productive work or of essential costs of cultivation.

3.3.2 Non-institutional (Informal) Sources: These include moneylenders, pawnbrokers, savings collectors, money-guards, input supply shops. Because they know each other well and live in the same community, they understand each other's financial circumstances and can offer very flexible, convenient and fast services. These services can also be costly and the choice of financial products limited and very short-term.

Till Independence in 1947, money lenders and the landlords were the principal sources of rural credit. Over the years, the operations of moneylenders have declined in view of debt relief legislations, the system of licensing moneylenders and restrictions on the use and transfer of land as security. Similarly, the abolition of all privileged tenures, both in zamindari and ryotwari areas, has discouraged investment by the landlords and larger cultivators.

Historically, moneylenders have played a significant role in meeting the credit needs of the rural producers. With stringent laws against money lending and the phenomenal growth of the formal credit delivery system, it was thought that money lenders would soon be out of business. Instead they have been in the business of lending in several disguises.

There are two types of moneylenders in rural areas: (a) agriculturist moneylenders who carry on the business of money lending along with farming, and (b) professional moneylenders whose only occupation is money lending. Although the relative importance of moneylenders has declined over the years, they are still an important source of credit for the rural people, particularly the small farmers and the artisans.

Moneylenders usually charge higher rates from poorer borrowers than from less poor ones. While moneylenders are often demonized and accused of usury, their services are convenient and fast, and they can be very flexible when borrowers run into problems. Moneylenders are popular because, unlike government agencies, they give credit for every purpose. They are easily approachable by the credit seekers and there are not many formalities in transacting a loan. However, the malpractices adopted by the moneylenders to exploit the needy farmers cannot be overlooked. These malpractices pertain to charging of high rate of interest and adopting unfair means in the maintenance of accounts.

Perhaps influenced by traditional Western views about usury, the role of the traditional moneylender has been subject to much criticism, especially in the early stages of modern micro finance. As more poor people gained access to loans from micro credit institutions, it became apparent that the services of moneylenders continued to be valued. Borrowers were prepared to pay very high interest rates for services like quick loan disbursement, confidentiality and flexible repayment schedules. They do not always see lower interest rates as adequate compensation for the costs of attending meetings, attending training courses to qualify for disbursements or making monthly collateral contributions. They also find it distasteful to be forced to pretend they were borrowing to start a business, when they were often borrowing for other reasons (such as paying for school fees, dealing with health costs or securing the family food supply). The more recent focus on inclusive financial systems affords moneylenders more legitimacy, arguing in favour of regulation and efforts to increase competition between them to expand the options available to poor people.

It is true that the institutional sources of credit have weakened the hold of moneylenders on the rural masses. However, the benefits of institutional credit have not percolated to all sections of rural population. Landless workers and marginal farmers have not benefited adequately due to their ignorance of new sources of credit and also on account of their weak repaying capacity. These underprivileged rural sections still depend on the moneylenders and suffer their exploitative practices.

To sum up, it is imperative that the government takes initiatives to expand the network of institutional credit facilities in the rural areas and that the credit needs of the small and marginal farmers are met through earmarking credit for the group. Extension and marketing initiatives need to focus on this segment. At the same time, group initiatives need to be encouraged and awareness among the group has to be increased. The procedural formalities also have to be made less stringent to make the system more user-friendly for the largely illiterate group.

Given the distress among the farmers, it is important that a safety-net programme is introduced to ensure a minimum income for the farmers. Also the risk factor has to be mitigated through adequate insurance and credit facilities. At the same time, the outreach and efficiency of the institutional credit sources have to be improved. This is important to protect the small and marginal farmers who still heavily rely on private moneylenders who charge high interest rates and follow unscrupulous means to perpetuate indebtedness.

4

Rural Co-operative Credit Institutions

4.1 Co-operative Banks

Co-operative banks in India came into existence with the enactment of the Agricultural Credit Co-operative Societies Act in 1904. Co-operative banks form an integral part of the banking system in India. These banks operate mainly for the benefit of rural areas, particularly the agricultural sector. Co-operative banks mobilise deposits and supply agricultural and rural credit with a wider outreach. They are the main source of institutional credit to the farmers. Co-operative banks are chiefly responsible for breaking the monopoly of moneylenders in providing credit to agriculturists. They have also been an important instrument for various development schemes, particularly subsidy-based programmes for the poor. Co-operative banks operate for non-agricultural sector also but their role is small.

Though much smaller as compared to scheduled commercial banks, co-operative banks constitute an important segment of the Indian banking system. They have an extensive branch network and reach out to people in remote areas. They have traditionally played an important role in creating banking habits among the lower and middle-income groups and in strengthening the rural credit delivery system.

Unfortunately, financial reforms have not impacted the functioning of co-operative banks. This was brought out clearly in the following observation of the Reserve Bank of India, "Since the introduction of reforms, there has been very little perceptible improvement in either stability or efficiency of co-operative banks. In particular, the asset quality and profitability of scheduled urban co-operative banks (UCBs) showed some deterioration in the reform period. Positive impact of reforms, as has been witnessed in the case of commercial banking sector, may take longer to get manifested for co-operative banks given the late start of the reform process in this sector". [1]

The financial reforms process initiated in 1991 has tried to achieve regulatory convergence among various financial intermediaries in view of their systemic importance. Therefore, the basic objectives and instruments of reforms for co-operative banks have been the same as for state co-operative banks (SCBs). However, given the special characteristics of co-operative banks, they have been extended certain dispensations in terms of pace and sequencing of reforms.

4.1.1 Classification of Co-operative Banks: The co-operative banking structure in India comprises urban co-operative banks and rural co-operative credit institutions.

A. Urban Co-operative Banks (UCBs): UCBs consist of a single tier, *viz.* primary co-operative banks, commonly referred to as urban co-operative banks.

B. Rural Credit Co-operatives: Based on the nature of their lending operations, rural credit co-operatives have traditionally been bifurcated into two parallel wings: short-term and long-term.

4.2 Rural Credit Co-operatives

Co-operative credit societies form an integral part of the rural credit system in India. They are the main source of institutional credit to the farmers. These societies are chiefly responsible for breaking the monopoly of moneylenders in providing credit to the agriculturists. There are around 93,000 such societies in the country at present. In spite of their suitability and useful role in building up a just socio-economic rural life, co-operative societies suffer from various weaknesses. The heavy overdues of co-operative societies are a cause for concern. The rising overdues have reduced the borrowing and lending activities of these societies.

Moreover, these societies have paid inadequate attention to the needs of landless workers and rural artisans. Influential people in the villages have been the main beneficiaries of co-operative credit. Of late, there has been a tendency on the part of political leadership to write-off loans of the farmers. The RBI has repeatedly expressed concern in this regard because non-repayment of loans by the existing borrowers can adversely affect recycling of funds and the credit chances of the prospective borrowers.

4.2.1 Short-term Rural Credit Co-operatives: The short-term provide crop and other working capital loans to farmers and rural artisans primarily for short-term purposes. These credit institutions have a three-tier federal structure: (a) at the apex of the system is a state co-operative bank (SCB) in each State, (b) at the middle (or district) level, there are central co-operative banks (CCBs) also known as district co-operative banks, and (c) at the lowest (or village) level are the primary agricultural credit societies (PACS). The smaller States and Union Territories (UTs) have a two-tier structure with SCBs directly meeting the credit requirements of PACS.

A. State Co-operative Bank (SCB): SCB is the highest agency of the three-tier co-operative credit structure in a state. It serves as a link between RBI and the CCBs and PACS. The RBI provides credit to lower level co-operatives through the SCB. This function of the RBI has now been taken over by NABARD. The SCB also acts as a *balancing centre* for CCBs in the sense that surplus funds of some CCBs are made available to other needy CCBs. The SCB exercises general control and supervision over CCBs and PACS.

B. Central Co-operative Banks (CCBs): These banks act as a link between the SCB and the PACS. The main task of CCBs is to lend money to affiliated village primary societies. The CCBs are expected to attract deposits from the general public.

C. Primary Agricultural Credit Societies (PACS): These societies form the basic unit of the co-operative credit system in India. These voluntary societies based on the principle of one man one vote have posed challenge to the exploitative practices of the village moneylenders.

The farmers and other small-time borrowers come in direct contact with these societies. The success of the co-operative credit movement depends largely on the strength of these village level societies. There are around 93,000 such societies in the country at present.

As a result of the expansion of the activities of PACS, the role of moneylenders in providing credit to agriculturists has decreased over the years. A major objective of PACS is to serve the needs of weaker sections of the society. For this purpose, the people with limited means, particularly scheduled castes and scheduled tribes, are encouraged to become members of these societies. Government has promoted multi-purpose societies in tribal areas for the benefit of people living there.

4.2.2 Long-term Rural Co-operatives: The long-term provide typically medium and long-term loans for making investments in agriculture, rural industries and, in the recent period, housing. Generally, these co-operatives have the following two tiers:

A. State Co-operative Agriculture and Rural Development Banks (SCARDBs): These banks operate at the State level.

B. Primary Co-operative Agriculture and Rural Development Banks (PCARDBs): These banks operate at the *taluka/tehsil* level.

4.3 Rural Credit Co-operatives in Historical Perspective

Rural credit co-operatives in India were originally envisaged as a mechanism for pooling the resources of people with small means and providing them with access to different financial services. Democratic in features, the movement was also an effective instrument for development of degraded waste lands, increasing productivity, providing food security, generating employment opportunities in rural areas and ensuring social and economic justice to the poor and vulnerable.

The history of the co-operative credit movement in India can be traced back to 1904 when the Co-operative Societies Act was passed. In 1919, *co-operation* became a provincial subject. The Co-operative Planning Committee, 1945 found that a large number of co-operatives were "saddled with the problem of frozen assets because of heavy overdues in repayment".

The co-operative banks in India play an important role in catering to the banking needs of the rural population. Soon after Independence in 1947, the inadequacy of rural credit engaged the attention of the Government of India and the RBI. The agricultural credit system as it has emerged over the years is the result of both evolution and intervention, and symbolises the nation's response to the dissatisfaction with the discredited colonial credit delivery system.

The Reserve Bank of India Act, 1934 has specific provisions relating to agricultural credit. Section 54 of the RBI Act specifically authorised the creation of an Agricultural Credit Department within the RBI to deal not only with the rural credit but also with the long-term finance including refinance. Section 17 of the Act empowered it to provide agricultural credit through state co-operative banks or any other banks engaged in the business of agricultural credit.

The foundation for building a broader credit infrastructure for rural credit was laid down by the All India Rural Credit Survey (1954). The Committee of Direction that conducted the survey recommended the creation of National Agricultural Credit Fund, which was subsequently created by the RBI. The Agricultural Refinance Corporation (ARC) set up by the RBI in 1963 provided funds by way of refinance, but credit co-operatives still did not function too well. Decentralised credit planning through the Lead Bank Scheme was also introduced to spearhead the credit allocation for, *inter alia*, agricultural lending. In order to emphasise the developmental and promotional role assigned to the ARC in addition to refinancing, the ARC was renamed as the Agricultural Refinance and Development Corporation (ARDC) in 1975.

Despite all these efforts, the flow of credit to the agricultural sector failed to exhibit any appreciable improvement as the co-operatives lacked resources to meet the expected demand. To solve these problems, the regional rural banks (RRBs) were set up in 1975. In order to strengthen the institutional credit for agriculture and rural development, National Bank for Agriculture and Rural Development (NABARD) was set up on July 12, 1982. On its establishment, NABARD took over the entire functions of the ARDC, the refinancing functions of the RBI in relation to co-operatives and regional rural banks (RRBs).

The rural credit co-operative system has served as an important instrument of credit delivery in rural and agricultural areas. The separate structure of rural co-operative sector for long-term and short-term loans has enabled these institutions to develop as specialised institutions for rural credit delivery. At the same time, their federal structure has helped in providing support structure for the guidance and critical financing for the lower structure. These institutions have wide outreach with as many as 93,000 primary agricultural co-operative societies (PACS), the grass root organisation of the rural co-operative banking structure, operating in the country.

4.4 Primary Agricultural Credit Societies (PACS)

Primary agricultural credit societies (PACS) are the foundation of the co-operative credit system on which the superstructure of the short-term co-operative credit system rests. It is the PACS which directly interface with individual farmers, provide short-term and medium-term credit, supply agricultural inputs, distribute consumer articles and arrange for marketing of produce of its members through a co-operative marketing society.

PACS continue to rely heavily on external support and have not yet been able to become self-reliant in respect of resources through deposit mobilisation and internal accruals, affecting their growth and expansion of business activities.

PACS need to function as viable units responsive to the needs, aspirations and convenience of its members, particularly those belonging to the more vulnerable sections of the society. They must function effectively as well-managed and multi-purpose institutions mobilising the savings of the rural people and providing a package of services including credit, supply of agricultural inputs and implements, consumer goods, marketing services and technical guidance with focus on weaker sections.

Some of the critical challenges facing primary level co-operative credit institutions, apart from improving resource mobilisation, are the following.

1. Increasing diversification in business portfolio.
2. Improving volume of business.
3. Arresting decline in membership by the borrowers.
4. Reducing cost of management.
5. Correcting imbalances in loans outstanding.
6. Improving skills of the staff and imparting professionalisation.
7. Strengthening management information system (MIS).
8. Reducing involvement in non/less profitable business.

4.5 NABARD and the Co-operative Sector

National Bank for Agriculture and Rural Development (NABARD) provides refinance to state co-operative agriculture and rural development banks (SCARDBs), state co-operative banks (SCBs), regional rural banks (RRBs) and other financial institutions approved by the RBI. The ultimate beneficiaries of refinance from NABARD could be individuals, partnership concerns, companies, State-owned corporations or co-operative societies.

4.5.1 Credit Extended by NABARD: NABARD provides short-term credit facilities to SCBs in respect of eligible CCBs for the following purposes:

1. Financing seasonal agricultural operations.
2. Marketing of crops.
3. Pisciculture activities.
4. Production and marketing activities of primary weavers and other industrial co-operative societies.
5. Labour contract/forest labour co-operative societies.

6. Individual rural artisans through PCS.
7. Procurement, stocking and distribution of chemical fertilisers.
8. Approved agricultural, allied and other marketing activities.

Short-term credit limits are also sanctioned to SCBs on behalf of apex/regional weavers/other industrial societies for financing procurement and marketing and trading-in-yarn. Short-term limits are also provided to RRBs for financing seasonal agricultural operations, marketing of crops and pisciculture activities.

Medium-term facilities are also provided to SCBs and RRBs for converting short-term into medium-term loans and for approved agricultural investments.

Long-term loans are provided to the State Governments for contributing to the share capital of co-operative credit institutions.

4.6 Problems of Rural Co-operatives

Rural co-operatives form an integral part of the rural credit system in India. They are the main source of institutional credit to the farmers. These societies are chiefly responsible for breaking the monopoly of moneylenders in providing credit to the agriculturists. There are around 93,000 such societies in the country at present.

Despite the phenomenal outreach and volume of operations, the financial health of a very large proportion of rural credit co-operatives has deteriorated significantly. The institutions are beset with problems like low resource base, high dependence on external sources of funding, excessive governmental control, dual control, huge accumulated losses, imbalances, poor business diversification, low recovery etc. These institutions do not, therefore, inspire confidence among their existing and potential members, depositors, borrowers and lenders. Thus, there is a need to find ways for strengthening the co-operative movement and making it a well-managed and vibrant medium to serve the credit needs of rural India, especially the small and marginal farmers.

Moreover, these societies have paid inadequate attention to the needs of landless workers and rural artisans. Influential people in the villages have been the main beneficiaries of co-operative credit. Of late, there has been a tendency on the part of political leadership to write-off loans of the farmers. The RBI has repeatedly expressed concern in this regard because non-repayment of loans by the existing borrowers can adversely affect recycling of funds and the credit chances of the prospective borrowers. A national approach on this issue is required so that co-operative credit system may fulfil the task assigned to it.

The rural co-operative credit institutions are beset with many problems which include the following:

1. Low resource base.
2. High dependence on refinancing agencies.
3. Lack of diversification.
4. Huge accumulated losses.
5. Persistent non-performing assets (NPAs).
6. Low recovery levels.
7. Various other types of organisational weaknesses.

NABARD and the RBI, therefore, have been taking several supervisory and developmental measures in consultation with the Government of India for the revival of weak institutions and orderly growth of this important segment of the financial sector.

4.6.1 Triangular Regulation of Rural Co-operatives: In the case of the rural banking sector, apart from the presence of the Registrar of Co-operative Societies for incorporation/registration-related regulation, banking regulation is further split between the RBI, which has the regulatory powers, and NABARD which is vested with the supervisory responsibility. The shortcomings of this segregation of regulatory and supervisory roles is compounded by the fact that NABARD has limited powers of enforcement of its supervisory findings, for which it has to depend on either its own persuasiveness or seek action through interventions by the RBI or the State Government.

The *duality of control* over the co-operative institutions is a contentious issue. The Task Force on Co-operative Credit System (Chairman: Jagdish Capoor), 1999 addressed the issue of duality of control over co-operative credit institutions and suggested to remove the overlap of controls and endowing functional autonomy and operational freedom to co-operatives. The Task Force suggested to draw an Action Plan to redefine the roles and responsibilities and areas of regulation through delegation of powers in respect of all the players in the field, *viz.* the State Government, RBI, NABARD and co-operative institutions. In view of the weaknesses persisting in the co-operative banks, a system of preparation of institution-specific development action plans and execution of Memorandum of Understanding have been initiated since 2003-04.

4.7 Regulatory Framework and Supervision

4.7.1 Asset Classification for State Government Guaranteed Advances: Revised guidelines on asset classification norms for State Government guaranteed exposures (i.e. advances and investments), as applicable to commercial banks, were issued to SCBs and CCBs on January 20, 2005 which are to be implemented in a phased manner. Accordingly, it was decided to delink the asset classification and provisioning requirements in respect of State Government guaranteed loans and advances from invocation of State Government guarantee and treat such exposures for asset classification purpose in the same manner as applicable to exposures not guaranteed by the State Governments. However, with a view to enabling banks to have a smooth transition in the matter, the revised prudential norms in respect of State Government guaranteed exposures (i.e. both advances and investments) will be implemented in a phased manner in two stages.

With effect from the year ending March 31, 2006, State Government guaranteed advances and investments in State Government guaranteed securities would attract asset classification and provisioning norms, if interest and/or instalment of principal or any other amount due to the bank remains overdue for more than 180 days. In the second stage, which would begin from the year ending March 31, 2007, State Government guaranteed advance and investment in State Government guaranteed securities would attract asset classification and provisioning norms, if interest and/or instalment of principal or any other amount due to the bank remains overdue for more than 90 days.

4.7.2 Additional Provisioning Requirement for NPAs: For the sake of convergence in policies governing all banks, guidelines for additional provisioning for all advances classified as *doubtful for more than three years* were issued on March 1, 2005, to be implemented in a phased manner from April 1, 2007.

In terms of the guidelines, for the unsecured portion of the advance, which is not covered by the realisable value of tangible security to which the bank has a valid recourse and the realisable value is estimated on a realistic basis, provision will be to the extent of 100 percent, as hitherto. The secured portion, on the other hand, would be divided into two categories. Outstanding stock of NPAs classified as *doubtful for more than three years* as on March 31, 2007 would need to be provided for in a phased manner up to 100 percent till March 31, 2010. Also, 100 percent provisioning would need to be made for the advances classified as *doubtful for more than three years* on or after April 1, 2007.

4.7.3 Prudential Guidelines on Agricultural Advances: As mentioned in the Annual Policy Statement of the RBI for the year 2004-05, prudential norms on income recognition, asset classification and provisioning with respect to agricultural advances were modified on July 12, 2004 with a view to aligning the repayment dates with harvesting of crops. Accordingly, effective September 30, 2004 a loan granted for short duration crops is required to be treated as NPA if the instalment of the principal or interest thereon remains unpaid for two crop seasons beyond the due date. A loan granted for long duration (with crop season longer than one year) crops is required to be treated as NPA, if the instalment of principal or interest thereon remains unpaid for one crop season beyond the due date.

4.7.4 Inspections: NABARD undertakes inspection of RRBs, SCBs and CCBs in accordance with the powers vested under Section 35(6) of the Banking Regulation Act, 1949 (AACS). Besides, NABARD conducts voluntary inspection of SCARDBs, Apex Weavers' Co-operative Societies and State Co-operative Marketing Federations.

The frequency of statutory/voluntary inspections by NABARD was increased from 2005-06. The statutory inspections of CCBs and RRBs with positive net worth as also the voluntary inspections of Apex Co-operative Societies/Federations would continue to be conducted once in two years. With the introduction of annual inspections, the system of conducting quick inspections has been dispensed with.

The Board of Supervision (BoS) constituted by NABARD in 1999 to provide guidance and direction on matters relating to supervision of SCBs, CCBs and RRBs meets periodically and deliberates on such issues as listed below.

1. Review of insolvent SCBs and CCBs.
2. State-wise review of the functioning of co-operative credit institutions.
3. Review of off-site supervisory system (OSS).
4. Review of frauds, misappropriation, embezzlements, and defalcations.
5. Review of functioning of StCBs and SCARDBs based on inspection findings.
6. Procedure for receipt and follow-up of compliance reports on inspection findings.
7. Risk management systems in co-operative banks and RRBs.
8. Review of financial position of RRBs with deposit erosion of 25 percent or more.

4.8 Task Force on Revival of Rural Co-operative Credit Institutions

The Government of India had constituted this Task Force (Chairman: A. Vaidyanathan), 2005 to propose an action plan for reviving the rural co-operative banking institutions and suggest an appropriate regulatory framework for these institutions. The Task Force in its Report submitted to the Central Government on February 15, 2005 made several recommendations to strengthen the rural co-operative credit structure in the country.

Major recommendations of the Task Force were as under:

1. Co-operative credit structure (CCS) is impaired in governance, managerial and financial fronts and hence needs to be revived and restructured.
2. Financial restructuring should be contingent on commitment to and implementation of legal and institutional reforms by the State Governments.
3. Financial assistance should be made available for: (a) wiping out accumulated losses, (b) covering invoked but unpaid guarantees given by the State Governments, (c) increasing the capital to a specified minimum level, (d) retiring Government share capital, and (e) technical assistance.
4. Availability of financial assistance from the Government of India should be strictly subject to legal and institutional reforms in the co-operative sector to ensure that the co-operatives become truly democratic and member-driven.
5. The Task Force also recommended certain major amendments to the provisions of the Banking Regulation Act, 1949 enabling removal of dual control and bringing the co-operatives under the regulatory control of the RBI.
6. Total financial assistance was estimated tentatively at ₹ 14,839 crore. The Task Force, however, recommended a special audit to ascertain the exact requirement of assistance. The financial assistance should be shared by the Government of India, State Governments and the CCS, based on the origin

of losses within a flexible matrix.

7. NABARD should be designated as the nodal *implementing and pass through agency* to co-ordinate and monitor the progress of the programme representing the Government of India. NABARD should prepare model MoUs, model balance sheet proforma for PACS and CCBs.

4.9 Advisory Committee on the Flow of Credit to Agriculture and Related Activities from the Banking System, 2004

As indicated in its mid-term review of November 2003, the RBI constituted this Advisory Committee (Chairman: V.S. Vyas) which submitted its interim report in April 2004 and the final report in June 2004. It made the following recommendations:

1. A review of mandatory lending to agriculture by commercial banks to enlarge direct lending programmes.
2. Public and private sector banks should increase their direct agricultural lending to 12 percent of net bank credit in the next two years and to 13.5 percent two years thereafter, within the overall limit of 18.0 percent of total agricultural lending.
3. Banks should increase their disbursements to small and marginal farmers under Special Agricultural Credit Plan (SACP) to 40 percent by March 2007.
4. SACP to be restricted to direct lending and extended to private sector banks.
5. Reduction in cost of agricultural credit by enhancing the cost effectiveness of agricultural loans.
6. NPA norms for agricultural credit to be aligned with crop seasons. Loans for allied activities to be classified as NPA after 180 days of default. Credit flow to small borrowers to be improved through reduction in cost of borrowing, revolving credit packages, procedural simplification, involvement of Panchayati Raj institutions and micro finance.
7. SAA to be modified to remove rigidities. SAA to be mandatory only for Government sponsored programmes and the format of village surveys to be changed in view of

the current realities.

Based on the recommendations contained in the interim report of the Vyas Committee, the RBI, in its Annual Policy Statement for 2004-05, announced a number of measures to improve credit delivery to agriculture. These included: (a) treating loans to storage units designed to store agricultural products, irrespective of location, as indirect credit to agriculture, (b) treating investment by banks in securitised assets representing lending to agriculture as direct (indirect) lending to agriculture and (c) waiver of margin/security requirement for agricultural loans up to ₹ 50,000 and in case of agri-business and agri-clinics for loans up to ₹ 5 lakh. In addition, RBI also aligned repayment dates with harvesting of crops by treating loans granted for short duration crops as NPA, if the instalment of the principal or interest thereon remains unpaid for two crop seasons beyond the due date. Loans granted for long duration crops are treated as an NPA, only if the instalment of the principal or interest thereon remains unpaid for one crop season beyond the due date.

As recommended by the Advisory Committee, RBI announced that micro finance institutions would not be permitted to accept public deposits, unless they comply with the extant regulatory framework. The recommendation relating to service area approach (SAA) was accepted and an announcement to this effect was made in the RBI's mid-term review of Annual Policy Statement for 2004-05.

In connection with implementation of the recommendations of the Vyas Committee, the *Economic Survey, 2005-06* observed, "Continuing its endeavour to enhance the flow of credit to agriculture by removing delivery bottlenecks, the RBI, together with NABARD, implemented most of the recommendations of the Advisory Committee on Flow of Credit to Agriculture and Related Activities from the Banking System (Chairman: V.S. Vyas). Out of 99 recommendations made by the Committee, 33 were accepted and implemented by October 2005. These related to the following matters.

1. Procedural modifications and rationalisation of systems and procedures.
2. Tie-ups with related farm machinery manufacturers by banks.
3. Use of a flexible revolving credit limit to small borrowers of production or investment loans for meeting temporary shortfalls in family cash flows.
4. Co-opting joint liability group (JLG) and self-help group (SHG) approaches in addressing issues relating to financing oral lessees.
5. Addressing delays/refusal in opening savings bank accounts of SHGs.
6. Improving staffing in the rural areas to promote retail lending to agriculture.
7. Use of individual volunteers, farmers' clubs, NGOs or SHGs as direct selling agents.
8. Building synergy between good working primary agricultural credit societies and commercial banks.
9. Use of IT in rural branches.
10. Working out appropriate incentive structure for prompt repayment.
11. Making the rates of interest on small loans reasonable.
12. Improving the efficiency of credit delivery to small borrowers and association with contract farming.

Furthermore, some of the recommendations, *viz.*, stepping up credit for marketing and introduction of negotiable warehousing receipt system, support of State Governments for collecting dues, reduction of stamp duty on agricultural loans, legal amendments to Agricultural Produce Marketing Committee (APMC) Act by the State Governments, amendment to NABARD Act for operational autonomy, which were referred to the Government of India for examination, have been accepted". [2]

4.10 Expert Group on Investment Credit in Agriculture, 2005

With a view to increasing the flow of credit to agriculture, the RBI set up this Expert Group (Chairman: Y.S.P. Thorat) to formulate a strategy for increasing investment credit in agriculture. The Group in its Report submitted in June 2005 identified several factors which constrain growth in investment in agriculture. These included the following.

1. Meagre growth in minor irrigation and farm mechanization.
2. Declining public sector investment.
3. Limited credit absorptive capacity.
4. Lack of effective mechanism for technology transfer and poor extension services.
5. Inadequate extension services.
6. Limited infrastructure for agro processing, storage, value addition and marketing.
7. Restrictions on purchases outside the *mandis*.
8. Weather aberrations and output price fluctuations.
9. Inadequate risk mitigation mechanism.
10. Non-availability of land records.

The Group emphasised the need to accelerate investment in agriculture in order to achieve the desired level of growth. It also highlighted the need for investments to be appropriately structured, timed and well implemented in order to attain maximum effectiveness.

Major recommendations of the Group are set out below.

1. In view of various changes in the Indian rural canvas over the past few years, there is need for a shift in the thrust areas for investment credit to agriculture. Apart from the traditional investments such as land development and irrigation, increased focus needs to be accorded to the entire supply chain management of agriculture products, reform of agriculture markets and public management in agricultural infrastructure.
2. State Governments need to lay emphasis on legal provisions/computerisation of land records, legal support for recovery, reforms in agricultural marketing, improving credit absorptive capacity through supporting infrastructure, strengthening infrastructure, improving extension network

and developing marketing links.

3. NABARD should take special steps to facilitate capacity building of credit institutions in appraisal skill, particularly in North-Eastern States, and design appropriate products for financing rural infrastructure projects outside the RIDF by mobilising resources from the market or banks at competitive rates of interest.
4. Water management policies and investment in water conservation be designed jointly by the State Governments and banks for improving productivity in agriculture.
5. The State Governments and NABARD should make investments in participatory community projects and in soil treatment to make wasteland and fallow land cultivable.

4.11 Working Group on Warehouse Receipts and Commodity Futures, 2005

In pursuance of the announcement made in the Mid-term Review of Annual Policy Statement for the year 2004-05, the RBI constituted this Working Group (Chairman: Prashant Saran) with a view to examining the role of banks in providing loans against warehouse receipts and evolving a framework for participation of banks in the commodity futures market. The Working Group in its Report submitted in April 2005 recommended that banks may be permitted to offer futures-based products to farmers in order to enable them to hedge against price risk.

The Working Group was entrusted with the task of evolving broad guidelines, criteria, limits, risk management system as also a legal framework for facilitating participation of banks in commodity (derivative) market and use of warehouse receipts in financing of agriculture. The major recommendations of the Group are set out below.

1. Considering the experience that banks already have in dealing with agricultural commodities, it would be prudent at the current stage to permit banks to deal with derivatives in agricultural commodities only.

2. A system needs to be evolved by which warehouse receipts become freely transferable between holders as it would reduce transaction costs and increase usage.
3. An umbrella structure, which may act as a closed user group (CUG) for everyone engaged in the agricultural commodities business, be created. The umbrella structure is envisaged as an electronic platform that would offer straight through processing for everyone connected with commodities. There can be more than one CUG which would be subject to regulation and supervision by a regulatory authority such as Forward Markets Commission (FMC).
4. Proprietary positions in agricultural commodity derivatives could be used by banks to mitigate their risk in lending to farmers. To achieve this, they will have to buy options on futures.
5. The Forward Contracts (Regulation) Act, 1952 be amended and the FMC should evolve a framework for introducing "options" trading in agricultural commodities in India.
6. Banks may be permitted to have independent proprietary position in commodity futures linked in a macro way to their credit portfolio. However, suitable risk control measures may have to be adopted by banks.
7. At present, purely cash-settled contracts are not available in India. The banks trading or dealing in commodity contracts should, therefore, be prepared to make or accept delivery of physical goods. While no restriction may be placed in this regard, banks may be persuaded to preferably close their positions and cash settle the contracts.
8. Banks may be granted general permission to become professional clearing members of commodity exchanges subject to the condition that they do not assume any exposure risk on account of offering clearing services to their trading clients. At least for the present, banks may not be permitted to act as trading members in the commodity exchanges.

9. While banks may continue to hold their equity stake in the commodity exchanges in order to provide them financial strength and stability, they may reduce/divest their equity holding to a maximum permitted level of 5 percent over a period of time so as to avoid any conflict of interest.

To sum up, historically, rural co-operative credit institutions (or simply rural co-operatives) have played an important role in providing institutional credit to the agricultural and rural sectors. The structure of rural co-operative banks is not uniform across all the States of the country. Some States have a unitary structure with the State level banks operating through their own branches, while others have a mixed structure incorporating both unitary and federal systems.

India is a country with a population of 121 crore (2011 Census) of which around 70 percent resides in around 6 lakh villages. There are around 93,000 PACS in the country. On grounds of outreach, co-operatives cannot be ignored. The outreach is significant not merely in absolute numbers but also in terms of location of outlets. The number of PACS located in hilly terrains, deserts and other areas with poor access far exceed the number of rural branches of commercial banks and RRBs. Though the network of commercial banks and RRBs has spread rapidly, their reach in the countryside both in terms of the number of clients and accessibility to the small and marginal farmers and other poorer segments is far less than that of co-operatives.

In spite of their suitability and useful role in building up a just socio-economic rural life, co-operative societies suffer from various weaknesses and their performance has been far from satisfactory in certain respects. The heavy overdues of co-operative societies are a cause for concern. The rising overdues have reduced the borrowing and lending activities of these societies. The increasing incidence of defaulting has brought bad name to these societies.

Co-operative societies have paid inadequate attention to the needs of landless workers and the rural artisans. The influential people in the villages have been the main beneficiaries of co-operative credit. Of late, there has been a tendency on the part of political leadership to write off the loans of the farmers. The RBI has repeatedly expressed concern in this regard because the non-repayment of loans by the existing borrowers adversely affects recycling of funds and the credit chances of prospective borrowers. A national approach on this issue is required so that co-operative credit system may fulfil the task assigned to it.

Positive impact of reforms, as has been witnessed in the case of commercial banking sector, may take longer to get manifested for co-operative banks given the late start of the reform process in this sector. Unless such a positive scenario evolves for the co-operative banking sector in the near future, the financial health of many of these banks would continue to remain a cause of concern.

Endnotes

1. Reserve Bank of India, *Report on Currency and Finance,* 2001-2002, p. VI-18.
2. Government of India, *Economic Survey, 2005-06*, p. 63.

5

Regional Rural Banks (RRBs)

Regional rural banks (RRBs) form an important segment of the rural financial sector. They were conceived as institutions that combine the local feel and familiarity of the co-operatives with the business capabilities of commercial banks. This sector has an exclusive role in improving financial inclusion and catering to vital sectors like agriculture and allied economic activities. Public policy, therefore, aims at keeping this sector viable and strong through various forms of active intervention.

RRBs were introduced and promoted by the Government of India with the noble objective of promoting savings habits and providing credit delivery mechanism to the rural India. The target groups were small and marginal farmers, agricultural labourers, artisans and small entrepreneurs for development of agriculture, trade, industry and other commercial activities in rural India. RRBs have wide reach in rural India and with their region-centric banking activities and closer relationship with the local authorities and population, they were expected to provide necessary banking infrastructure. They have been successful in mobilizing small savings in the rural sector.

Setting up of RRBs in the mid-1970s was a major initiative to meet credit requirements of rural people. The RRBs are specialized rural financial institutions for developing the rural economy by providing credit to small and marginal farmers, agricultural labourers, artisans and small entrepreneurs. During the 40 years of existence of RRBs, several Working Groups and Committees were set up at various points of time to deliberate on issues relating to RRBs and suggest measures to address the same. The focus has varied over time depending on the immediate concerns and the prevailing policy regime. While some of the issues relating to RRBs have lost their significance over time, others have become more relevant.

5.1 Nature and Objectives of RRBs

Agriculture and rural sectors play an important role in India's overall development strategy in terms of income and employment generation and poverty alleviation. Great significance has, therefore, been accorded to developing appropriate institutions and mechanisms for catering to the credit requirements of these sectors.

Despite the measures taken by the Government of India and the RBI—including nationalisation of 14 major commercial banks in 1969—a large proportion of the rural poor continued to be outside the banking fold. A Working Group (Chairman: M. Narasimham) was set up in 1975 to explore the possibilities of evolving an alternative rural credit agency to benefit the rural poor. The Group recommended formation of a new set of regionally-oriented rural banks which would combine the local feel and familiarity of rural problems characteristic of cooperatives and the professionalism and large resource base of commercial banks. RRBs were set up as a sequel to this recommendation.

RRBs have a special place in the multi-agency approach adopted to provide agricultural and rural credit in India. These banks were established under the Regional Rural Banks Act, 1976 "with a view to developing the rural economy by providing, for the purpose of development of agriculture, trade, commerce, industry and other productive activities in the rural areas, credit and other facilities, particularly to small and marginal farmers, agricultural labourers, artisans and small entrepreneurs, and for matters connected therewith and incidental thereto".

The capital of RRBs is contributed by the Union Government, concerned State Government and a sponsor bank in the ratio 50:15:35. RRBs have played a key role in rural institutional financing in terms of geographical coverage, clientele outreach, business volume and contribution to the development of the rural economy.

Besides the RRBs, commercial and co-operative banks have been catering to the credit requirements of the rural sector. While the commercial banks, with their focus on profitability had certain limitations in accelerating agricultural credit, the cooperative banks efforts were also hampered by several financial weaknesses.

Though over the years the RRBs have been able to expand their outreach and business and meet the credit requirements of the poor, several weaknesses have emerged, eroding their profitability and viability. The recent focus of the Government of India on doubling the flow of credit to the agricultural sector has warranted a re-look at the relative roles of co-operative banks, RRBs and commercial banks.

As the very objective of setting up RRBs was to extend adequate credit to the rural borrowers and particularly the economically weaker sections, owing to their rural orientation, there is a growing realization that RRBs could be used as an effective vehicle for credit delivery in the rural areas. There is, therefore, a need to devise ways and means to improve the health and viability of RRBs so as to reposition them in the credit delivery mechanism in India.

5.2 Amalgamation of RRBs

RRBs have been in sharp focus over the last few years with several measures initiated towards strengthening them and making them vibrant channels of credit delivery, particularly for the rural sector. The most prominent of these has been the process of state-wise amalgamation of RRBs sponsored by the same sponsor bank. As a result of the process of amalgamation, initiated in 2005, the number of RRBs in the country declined from 196 to 96 at the end of March 2007 to 56 at the end of March 2015. Presently, 43 RRBs are functioning in the country.

The structural consolidation of RRBs has resulted in formation of new RRBs, which are financially stronger and bigger in size in terms of business volume and outreach. They will thus be able to take advantages of the economies of scale and reduce their operational costs. With the advantages of local feel and familiarity acquired by the RRBs, they would now be in a better position to achieve the objectives of rural development and financial inclusion.

5.3 Autonomy for RRBs

Further, measures have been taken to provide greater autonomy to RRBs and enlarge their business activities. A majority of the recommendations of the Task Force on Empowering RRB Boards for Operational Efficiency (Chairman: K.G. Karmakar) have already been implemented. RRBs have also been allowed to open currency chests, conduct State government business as sub-agents of sponsor banks, take up corporate agency business without risk participation for distribution of all types of insurance products and open foreign currency non-resident (FCNR) accounts, subject to certain conditions. The branch licensing procedure for RRBs has been simplified with powers now delegated to the regional offices of Reserve Bank of India. The branch licensing policy has also been liberalised and the norms for opening new branches in hitherto uncovered districts have been relaxed. As a result, there has been a rapid increase in the number of branches of RRBs.

5.4 RRBs as Vehicles of Financial Inclusion

RRBs have the potential to play a greater role in financial inclusion primarily because of their strategic geographical location in remote places in the country. In certain parts of the country, e.g. in the states of UP, Bihar and North-Eastern regions, the banking system mainly exists in the form of RRBs. Recognising the importance of achieving inclusive growth in the country, the RBI has permitted banks to utilise the services of non-governmental organizations (NGOs), self-help groups (SHGs), micro finance institutions (other than non-banking financial companies) and other civil society organisations as intermediaries to provide financial and banking services through the use of business facilitator and business correspondent (BC) models. The BC model allows banks to do 'cash-in-cash-out' transactions at a location much closer to the rural population, thus addressing the last mile problem. However, customers in many parts of the country have to travel long distances, spend on transportation costs besides sacrificing their daily wages to visit the banks for doing their routine banking transactions and such inaccessibility contributes to the dormancy of many accounts in RRBs as well.

The objective of financial inclusion would be fully achieved if RRBs are able to bring banking to the door step of the customers just as the commercial banks have started taking such initiatives. It is here that the large scale usage of information and communication technology (ICT) solutions lends support. RRB presence in rural areas leveraged by ICT would considerably enhance their reach, and delivery of banking services to the remote corners of the country.

The Committee on Financial Inclusion (Chairman: C. Rangarajan), also emphasised the role of IT and banking correspondents on a larger scale for achieving financial inclusion. The Committee envisaged that RRBs may extend services to unbanked areas and increase their credit to deposit ratio. The need for setting target for microfinance and financial inclusion was also envisaged. The Committee also recommended 100 percent financial inclusion of the large number of hitherto excluded farm households in order to reduce their indebtedness to the unregulated/informal sector.

The Committee estimated that 51.4 percent of the farm households do not get any credit from formal or informal sources. The North-Eastern Region, Eastern Region and Central Region taken together, account for 68 percent of the farm households having no access to credit.

The reach of RRBs particularly in regions and across population groups facing the brunt of financial exclusion is impressive. In rural areas, RRBs account for a substantial 37 percent of total offices of all scheduled commercial banks. In semi-urban areas, their share comes to 15 percent. With the process of merger strengthening, to some extent, the viability of the RRBs and also because of the local feel and familiarity they command, RRBs are in a unique position to play a very useful role in financial inclusion.

RRBs need to be encouraged and supported in their financial inclusion initiatives for, inter alia, the following reasons:

1. Have presence in most of districts of the country.
2. Stronger presence in NER, ER and Central Regions.
3. Essential particularly for the areas where the financial exclusion rate is quite high.
4. Higher concentration of rural and semi-rural branches.
5. Have potential for intake of many more small accounts.
6. Though there are 43 RRBs with relatively reasonable performance, their net worth is not high and thus majority of RRBs are not financially very sound.

5.5 Factors Influencing the Performance of RRBs

Since their inception, the financial health of RRBs has been indifferent. A host of factors, both internal and external, have had a bearing on the performance of RRBs. Some of the major factors that had a bearing on the performance of RRBs are as follows:

5.5.1 Area of Operation and Clientele Base: The RRBs are constrained in their operations by their limited area of operation. This coupled with their narrow base of business activities and the low clientele base, has resulted in high risk exposure of RRBs. The customers of RRBs comprise small and marginal farmers, small-scale sector, small transport operators, SHGs, etc., whose credit requirements are mostly small. RRBs are unable to cross-subsidise their lending business as they do not generally provide credit to wealthy borrowers with large needs, thereby affecting their capacity to earn higher incomes.

There has been an uneven growth of RRBs due to the diffusion in the perceived objectives of RRBs over time. Despite the pressures of credit expansion, improvement in recovery performance, profit orientation and strict compliances to banking norms, the general perception has been that RRBs have got only social objectives, without any viability consideration, which has to be changed.

5.5.2 Capital Base and Organisational Structure: RRBs as a group have a low capital base, and their authorised capital of ₹ 1 crore places serious limitations on their business size. Furthermore, in the case of some of the RRBs their deposit liabilities are very large compared to their capital base. In view of their low capital base, in the event of inefficient use/misuse of funds resulting in a financial problem, the stakeholders would have to bail out the bank.

The size of financial assets, as well as linkages which are necessary for effective banking services has been limited by the small organizational structure of RRBs. This has also come in the way of growth in business volumes and garnering a larger share of the rural financial market.

5.5.3 Loan Delinquencies: RRBs loan recovery rates have declined over the years, resulting in a large over hang of NPAs which has come in their way of recycling funds and increasing the flow of credit to the rural sector. The directed lending policy for RRBs has resulted in low quality of assets. This coupled with high cost of funds and below cost interest rates on loans has led to high accumulated losses and piling up of bad assets in the case of many RRBs.

It is noteworthy that the target rural group has been one of the weaker and lowest strata of the Indian society. Smaller and marginal farmers and agricultural labourers always run short of money even for meeting their daily needs of life. Given the fact that most the villages in India still does not have clean drinking water and sanitation facilities, top it with lack of basic health facilities, makes them one of the most vulnerable groups in

India. In any nature-made or man-made calamities, they are the most affected. Thus, credit facilities taken by the rural poor are mostly not utilized for specified productive objective for which it was made available. For instance, when an agricultural labourer takes a small loan from an RRB for the purpose of buying a cow, and only a small portion of it is utilized for the stated purpose, the remaining amount is used for household needs or for tending to sick. Such misappropriation seems very common and ultimately the labourer who took the loan would be unable to repay it. This naturally leads to substantial non-performing and lost assets in RRBs.

5.5.4 Cost Structure and Poor Financial Management Skills: RRBs are characterized by high cost of servicing numerous small accounts and high wage cost. Furthermore, RRBs get credit from sponsor banks and refinance from NABARD at rates of interest higher than the market rates. This places limitations on their ability to reduce the rates they charge to their ultimate borrowers, although they are compelled to do so, on account of competition from banks.

Poor financial management skills, coupled with pressures from various quarters (like sponsor banks) appears to have resulted in inefficient allocation of resources by RRBs which in turn is reflected in the high incidence of NPAs and parking of large funds with sponsor banks.

5.5.5 Staff Structure: Limited exposure and lack of appropriate training, has resulted in RRBs staff lacking the necessary skills and capacity to cater to the changing requirements of the rural sector. Furthermore, the ban on recruitment has also resulted in ageing staff structure constraining efficiency in operations. Uniform norms and personnel policies have been applied to RRBs through out the country ignoring local touch thereby causing staff unrest, poor industrial relations, innumerable litigations and lowering of staff morale as also their involvement with the development tasks.

The chairmen of most of the RRBs are from sponsor banks, which limits the freedom and decision making capacity of the RRBs. Even for small matters RRBs have to refer to their sponsor banks, which leads to delay in decision-making and reduces efficiency. Furthermore, the board of directors of RRBs may not always function effectively as some of the members do not have necessary skills and expertise to take important financial decisions.

5.5.6 Dependence on Sponsor Banks: Another weakness observed in the case of RRBs is their failure to adequately integrate with the financial markets of the country due to their heavy dependence on sponsor banks for financial/business initiatives. RRBs are also some times perceived as potential competitors, due to the presence of the sponsor banks in the same area of operation. Despite the best intentions at the policy levels in sponsor banks, the RRBs have suffered at the ground level wherever there has been any conflict of business interests of RRBs and their sponsor banks. RRBs have therefore, not been able to establish systems and procedures required for providing efficient services to their clients, as also for efficient management of their financial resources.

Besides the above, functioning of RRBs has also been affected by certain legacy problems and policy constraints. The administered interest rate regime prevalent in the system for a considerably long time influenced the performance of RRBs. These banks were required to lend at low interest rates as they were financing the weaker sections and at the same time allowed to pay a slightly higher rate of interest on deposits.

The RRBs were required to maintain their local character or flavour with a view to identifying more with the rural populace. This was initially embedded in the wage structure designed for these banks. However, the change in the wage structure of RRBs by bringing them on par with the commercial banks led to higher wage costs, thereby affecting the performance of these banks.

5.6 Restructuring of RRBs

In order to reposition RRBs as an effective instrument of

credit delivery in the Indian financial system, an Internal Working Group on RRBs (Chairman: A.V. Sardesai) was set up by the RBI in February 2005 to examine various alternatives available within the existing legal framework for strengthening the RRBs and making them viable rural financial institutions. The Group, in its final report submitted in June 2005, made several recommendations for restructuring the RRBs. The main recommendations of the Working Group related to restructuring options, change of sponsor banks, minimum capital requirements, governance and management, regulation and supervision.

The major recommendations of the Group were as follows:

1. To improve the operational viability of RRBs, the route of merger/amalgamation of RRBs may be considered along two lines: (a) merger between RRBs of the same sponsor bank in the same State, and (b) merger of RRBs sponsored by different banks in the same State.
2. A change in sponsor banks may, in some cases, help improve competitiveness, work culture and efficiency of concerned RRBs for which new banks, both public and private sector, could be considered.
3. Merged entities and existing RRBs that have accumulated losses can be capitalised to wipe out the losses and satisfy minimum capital requirement. The CRAR may initially be kept at 5 percent.
4. For those RRBs which may not turn around within a specified time limit, say 3 to 5 years, an exit route may be considered subject to extant legal provisions.
5. Process of appointment of Chairmen of RRBs may be re-examined to explore the possibility of appointing them from the open market through a transparent process.
6. Boards of RRBs may be strengthened by making them broad-based through inclusion of professionals such as agricultural experts, bankers etc.
7. An appropriate recruitment policy, providing for greater flexibility and freedom, may be required for RRBs.

8. An appropriate incentive structure, career planning, relevant training, especially in skill upgradation and information technology, be evolved for employees of RRBs.
9. It would be appropriate if both the regulatory and supervisory functions relating to RRBs are exercised by the RBI.
10. RRBs may be encouraged to actively consider distribution of products of mutual fund/insurance companies, rationalisation of branch network, participate in consortium lending within their areas of operations.
11. RRBs may be considered for currency chest facility and empowered to collect taxes by the State Governments.

5.7 Manpower Challenges of RRBs

Measures have also been taken to address the manpower challenges in the RRBs. It is known that RRBs do not have their own training establishments so far. The existing training facilities available for RRB staff are Bankers Institute for Rural Development, Lucknow, College of Agricultural Banking, Pune, regional training colleges of NABARD at Mangalore and Bolpur, and the sponsor bank training institutes. However, all these institutions (other than sponsor bank training institutes) provide training only to officers and not to clerical or subordinate staff.

The Committee to Formulate a Comprehensive Human Resource Policy for RRBs (Chairman: Y.S.P. Thorat), had, in its report recommended that RRBs should have an exclusive training cell within the Personnel Department at Head Office and bestow more attention to the training function. It also recommended that sponsor banks can consider earmarking in any one training institute in a state, at least one channel to cater to the training requirements of all RRBs within the state and/or the adjoining states.

5.8 Computerisation in RRBs

The need for computerisation in RRBs had been felt since long and some RRBs had been taking some steps in that direction. In July 2001, Government of India and NABARD advised the RRBs to initiate immediate steps so that head office, area office and a minimum of 50 percent of the branches were computerised in a phased manner in the next 5 years. Sponsor banks were also advised to formulate RRB-wise Action Plans, keeping in view the financial position of RRBs, infrastructure facilities available in their command area and the business potential of the RRB branches. Necessary support to implement the programme was also required to come from the sponsor bank.

NABARD made a beginning by extending support to select RRBs by providing PCs, peripherals, standard software packages as also customised MIS package and training inputs under its Swiss Agency for Development and Cooperation (SDC) programme. A review made by NABARD in respect of 152 RRBs in 2005 indicated that only 9 banks had reported achieving 100 percent computerisation. Most of the RRBs were lagging behind the target of computerising 50 percent of their branches. The Task Force on Empowering RRBs for Operational Efficiency (Chairman: K.G. Karmakar) had made the following observations regarding the computerisation scenario in RRBs:

1. Level of computerisation is far behind schedule.
2. Even RRBs of same sponsor banks although following the same technology, are at different levels of computerisation due to varied financial health, environment, local conditions which has become a problem when such RRBs have been amalgamated.
3. Computerisation needs both capital and recurring expenses which are beyond the capability of some of the banks.
4. RRBs, which have progressed well, have adopted a particular technology mainly of the sponsor bank and invested sizeable amounts.
5. A few RRBs reaped the benefit of hosting their own website by way of mobilisation of deposits from non traditional segments.

6. A few of them established direct links with money market operators for investments.
7. Internet facilities have been used for faster communication with techno savvy customers and other agencies.

These observations highlighted the varying status of RRBs with regard to computerisation.

The status of computerisation at the end of March 2007 as reported by 76 of the 96 RRBs to the Committee to Formulate a Comprehensive Human Resource Policy for RRBs (Chairman: Y.S.P. Thorat) indicated that 35 of the reporting banks had achieved 100 percent computerisation while 25 banks had achieved 50 to 100 percent computerisation.

5.9 Working Group on Technology Upgradation of Regional Rural Banks, August 2008

In RBI's Mid-term Review of Annual Policy for 2007-08, it was stated that in order to prepare RRBs to adopt appropriate technology and migrate to core banking solutions (CBS) [1] for better customer services, it was proposed to constitute a Working Group with representatives from RBI, NABARD, sponsor banks and RRBs for preparing a road-map for migration to core banking solutions by RRBs.

Accordingly, a Working Group (Chairman: G. Srinivasan) was set up with the following terms of reference:

1. To determine the nature of core banking solutions required for RRBs having regard to the range of their business and customer service.
2. To examine various options including extending core banking solutions of the sponsor banks to their RRBs with necessary modifications and firewalls.
3. To estimate the likely costs involved and funding and training arrangements that may be necessary.
4. To draw out a time-bound road map for implementation.

The Working Group was also requested to examine the possibility of using solar power generating devices for meeting the power requirements of RRBs, especially in remote areas.

The Working Group was of the opinion that RRBs cannot afford to remain isolated from the technological developments sweeping the banking sector. With the commercial banks racing towards a higher degree of technological sophistication, the RRBs would be required to adopt technology for improving the quality of their customer service. However, given the different levels at which the different RRBs are presently placed in regard to their status of computerisation, a "one strategy fits all" approach may not be workable.

The Working Group was of the view that as a matter of policy, all RRBs should begin moving towards CBS. The CBS in RRBs should be geared towards better management control and monitoring, wider range of services offered and enhanced level of customer satisfaction. Adoption of CBS would lead to uniformity in work environment, more informed decision making, centralised processing and better MIS and reporting and improved regulatory compliance.

The Working Group also examined the use of solar power devices such as solar photovoltaic cells [2] for RRBs, particularly in respect of branches located in remote areas which are not assured of continuous power supply. In this context, the experience of one of the RRBs in Uttar Pradesh, which has made a beginning in this direction, was also studied.

Funding the cost of moving towards CBS is an important issue for RRBs, particularly as several RRBs continue to incur operating losses. Further, many RRBs still continue to have accumulated losses and even negative net worth. Despite this position, there are RRBs which are healthy and making sustained profits. The Working Group considered this aspect and was of the view that funding support may be provided to all RRBs in the matter of adopting CBS, irrespective of their financial position. This would enable the entire sector to move uniformly towards adopting CBSs.

A summary of the recommendations of the Working Group is given below.

1. The significant differences in the level of computerisation

between different RRBs need to be taken into account while preparing any plan for further technology upgradation of RRBs.

2. As a matter of policy, all RRBs should begin moving towards CBS. The CBS in RRBs should be geared towards better management control and monitoring, wider range of services offered and enhanced level of customer satisfaction. Adoption of CBS would lead to uniformity in work environment, more informed decision making, centralised processing and better MIS and reporting and improved regulatory compliance.
3. The respective sponsor banks may be given the option of selecting the service provider for their RRBs. This provider may be same as for the sponsor bank or different as per the requirement of the RRBs. In case a sponsor bank has developed its own software, it may consider making the same available to its RRBs.
4. Any technology platform for CBS needs to be reliable, scalable, easily available, manageable and secure. For this, the background, credentials and experience of the vendor are extremely important. It would therefore be prudent to rely on the trusted and established vendors to provide services to RRBs.
5. Sponsor banks must own major responsibility in taking RRBs on the path to CBS. However, the requirements of the RRBs have to be borne in mind as these banks may not require the full suite of services that are available in sponsor banks and hence a plain vanilla tailored to their needs should be provided.
6. RRB branches in remote areas where power is a serious problem may take recourse to powering their branches through solar power in a CBS scenario.
7. Funding support may be provided to all RRBs in the matter of adopting CBS, irrespective of their financial position. This would enable the entire sector to move uniformly towards adopting CBS.

8. While sponsor banks may contribute 25 percent of the cost required for taking their RRBs to CBS, the remaining cost may be borne by Reserve Bank through Institute for Development and Research in Banking Technology (IDRBT). The IDRBT, in turn would provide necessary funds to the sponsor banks for their sponsored RRBs. The support could be in the form of interest free loans, repayable in three years.
9. The training requirements of staff of RRBs on account of moving towards CBS would have to be met by sponsor banks through their training establishments. The sponsor banks should also meet the costs incurred in this regard.
10. The roll-out of the road map for implementation of CBS in RRBs should start at the earliest. RRBs in which 100 per cent branches are computerised, should implement CBS in all their branches by September 2009.
11. The remaining RRBs may also start the process of moving their branches to CBS at the earliest. Such RRBs should implement CBS in at least 25 percent of their branches by September 2009 and at least 50 percent of their branches by September 2010. The remaining branches may be endeavoured to be covered by September 2011. By that date, at least 90 percent of the business of the banks should be on CBS.
12. The responsibility of ensuring that the time frame suggested is adhered to would be that of the sponsor bank.
13. All new branches opened after September 2009 may be made CBS compliant from day 1.

To sum up, in spite of the various measures taken by the Government and the RBI through social control and the nationalisation of major commercial banks in 1969, a large proportion of the rural poor remained outside the banking fold. Therefore, the Government of India promoted regional rural banks (RRBs) through the RRBs Act of 1976 to bridge the gap in the flow of credit to the rural poor. The RRBs have a special place in the multi-agency approach adopted to provide agricultural and rural credit in India. These banks are state-sponsored, regionally based and rural-oriented.

RBI has been initiating several measures from time to time for facilitating better access to financial services and credit for the rural population. The regional rural banks (RRBs), since their inception, have played a vital role in taking banking to the rural masses, making available credit to weaker sections of society, mobilising and channelising rural savings towards productive activities and in generating employment opportunities in rural areas. During the last two years, RRBs have been provided greater flexibility in operations. Branch licensing norms have been made liberal and powers are delegated to the Regional Offices of the Reserve Bank. Further, the process of mergers of all RRBs of the same sponsor bank in the same State has been effected and the RRBs with negative net worth are in the process of being re-capitalised.

RRBs, with their wide outreach in rural India, region-centric banking activities and close relationship with the local authorities and population, were expected to cater to the credit requirements of the rural areas and provide necessary banking infrastructure. Though the RRBs have been able to mobilize small savings of the rural sector, they have been relatively less successful in enhancing the flow of credit to the targeted rural poor.

With their increasing strength and spread, RRBs would have to enlarge their client base and become the principal vehicles for financial inclusion and rural banking in the country. However, technological changes are sweeping the banking sector. In order to survive effectively in the present scenario, the RRBs would require to be adequately equipped in terms of technology to provide efficient customer service to their clientele. While the commercial banks have gone ahead in computerisation of their operations and most banks are in an advanced stage of implementing total core banking solutions (CBS), the RRBs are lagging behind in this area.

The expectations of the Central and the State Governments from the RRBs are also increasing. It is envisaged that RRBs are able to render the same quality of service that commercial banks are able to give to their clients. Further, the Government, in order to reduce intermediation and reach out directly to the beneficiaries under several of its programmes, proposes to reach these persons through the electronic mechanisms. It is thus becoming imperative for RRBs to become increasingly technologically sound so as to offer competitive services to their clients.

The renewed emphasis on agricultural and rural development by the Government of India would lead to a growing demand for different types of financial services in the rural areas, as financial needs of the rural economy becomes diversified. The present structure of rural credit may not be able to cater to the same. RRBs would be called upon to play a greater role in providing such services due to their rural character and feel. RRBs have to take over a larger share of credit disbursements calling for much larger resource mobilization, as also greater efforts for their institutional strengthening.

Endnotes

1. Although there is no formal definition of CBSs, the term has been in use during the last few years. The advancement in technology, especially internet and information technology, has led to a new way of doing business in banking. The technologies have cut down time, working simultaneously on different issues and increased efficiency. The platform where information and communication technology are merged to suit core needs of banking may be referred to as CBS. In CBS, computer software performs the core operations of banking like handling and recording of transactions, maintenance of passbooks, interest calculations on deposits and loans, maintaining customer records and generating reports and statements. The software is installed at bank branches and then interconnected by means of communication lines telephone, internet and satellite communication. It allows customers to transact with the bank from any branch if it has installed CBS. This new platform has changed the way of working of banks.

   In an ideal CBS scenario, all products, processes, channels and customer relationship management tools are integrated and administered via a central database of the bank with branches and channels as delivery points. This enables data integration for various purposes including regulatory reporting and internal MIS all at considerably lower cost. The new generation private sector banks were the first to adopt CBS technologies in India followed by a few public sector banks. Gradually, the same were adopted by most of the commercial banks as part of their computerisation processes.

As per the Report on Trend and Progress of Banking in India 2006-07, the process of computerisation in commercial banks was now reaching near completion for most of the banks. Public sector banks continued to expend large amounts on computerization and development of communication networks.

2. Solar photovoltaic cells convert the sun's energy into DC electricity using silicon cells called solar cells. When sunlight falls on the solar cells, a DC voltage is generated across the cell. The solar cell is connected to a battery through a charge controller and electrical energy is stored in the battery. From the energy stored in the battery, either a DC load or an AC load through inverter is operated.

6

Micro Finance, Self-help Groups (SHGs) and NABARD

Micro finance is a movement whose objective is a world in which as many poor and near-poor households as possible have permanent access to an appropriate range of high quality financial services, including not just credit but also savings, insurance, and fund transfers. Many of those who promote micro finance believe that such access will help poor people get out of poverty. For others, micro finance is a way to promote economic development, employment and growth through the support of micro entrepreneurs and small businesses.

6.1 Meaning and Salient Features of Micro Finance

Micro finance is the provision of a diverse range of financial services and products including small loans (micro credit), savings accounts, insurance, pensions and money transfers. These are designed to assist people living in poverty who are not able to access financial services in the mainstream banking sector because they have no collateral, formal identification or steady income.

Poor people borrow from informal moneylenders and save with informal collectors. They receive loans and grants from charities. They buy insurance from state-owned companies. They receive funds transfers through formal or informal remittance networks. It is not easy to distinguish micro finance from similar activities. It could be claimed that a government that orders state banks to open deposit accounts for poor consumers, or a moneylender that engages in usury, or a charity that runs a heifer pool are engaged in micro finance. Ensuring financial services to poor people is best done by expanding the number of financial institutions available to them, as well as by strengthening the capacity of those institutions. In recent years there has also been increasing emphasis on expanding the diversity of institutions, since different institutions serve different needs.

Salient features of micro finance are as under:

1. Borrowers are from the low-income group.
2. Loans are of small amount.
3. Loans are for short duration.
4. Loans are offered without collaterals.
5. Loans are generally given for income generation purpose.
6. Repayment frequency is high.
7. Loan terms vary, but once repaid, the money is recycled and lent out to someone else.

6.2 What is a Self-help Group (SHG)?

A self-help group (SHG) is a small voluntary association of 10-20 poor people from the same socio-economic background who come together for the purpose of addressing their common socio-economic problems through self-help and mutual-help. They collect small savings (thrift) on regular basis. Out of the pooled money, small interest bearing loans are given to the members and some amount is deposited with a bank regularly. The bank lends money for economic activities of the group without collateral security and at market rates. The savings of poor members are pooled resources saved with great difficulty. This hard-earned money is termed as *warm money.* The money obtained by the group from outsiders, i.e. banks, MFIs is termed as *cold money.*

Most self-help groups are located in India, though SHGs can also be found in other countries, especially in South Asia and Southeast Asia.

Members make small regular contributions over a few months until there is enough capital with the group to begin lending. Funds may then be lent back to the members or to others in the village for any purpose. In India, many SHGs are *linked* to banks for the delivery of micro credit.

SHGs are started by non-governmental organizations (NGOs) that generally have broad anti-poverty agendas. SHGs are seen as instruments for a variety of goals including empowering women, developing leadership abilities among poor people, increasing school enrolments, and improving nutrition and the use of birth control. Financial intermediation is generally seen more as an entry point to these other goals, rather than as a primary objective.

Self-help groups (SHGs) have been instrumental in initiating micro entrepreneurial activities among those poor people who have been neglected so far and far away from the process of social as well economic development. Self-help groups-bank linkage programme is responsible for developing banking habits among the poorest of the poor people.

The basic objective of self-help group is upliftment of poor people by means of micro economic activities so that the members get job opportunities, sustainable income and some assets for generation of regular income. There is tremendous enthusiasm in formation of the groups but care is not taken for their proper growth and survival.

The most significant contribution of SHGs is that they have been instrumental in building up enough confidence among the poor people and now they are ready to participate in the process of development. Many of these have been running fair price shops very successfully. A sizable number of the groups are working as caterers for the State Government-sponsored Mid-Day Meal Scheme. It is noteworthy that a good number of the SHGs have been marketing successfully the products of domestic as well as multinational corporations in remote rural areas.

Highlighting the importance of SHGs, the Twelfth Five Year Plan (2012-17) observed, "The banking system, with its larger overheads, is perhaps not best suited to deal with small credits. This is where self-help groups (SHGs) and similar collective guarantee credit schemes have a big role to play.

Micro finance institutions are another vehicle. There have been some unfortunate developments in the case of micro finance, but we must be alive to the danger of throwing the baby out with the bathwater. The Micro finance Regulation Act which has been introduced in Parliament will establish a regulatory framework which would allay suspicions and allow the industry to develop unhindered with due regulatory oversight. We do need other kinds of mezzanine financial agencies—SHGs, micro finance, cooperatives—which permit the banks an easier way to fund the capital needs of small creditors". [1]

6.3 Micro Finance and National Bank for Agriculture and Rural Development (NABARD)

Set up in 1982, National Bank for Agriculture and Rural Development (NABARD), is the apex institution accredited with all matters concerning policy, planning and operations in the field of credit for agriculture and other economic activities in rural areas in India. NABARD serves as an apex refinancing agency for the institutions providing investment and production credit in rural areas.

6.3.1 Establishment of NABARD: The Committee to Review Arrangements for Institutional Credit for Agriculture and Rural Development (CRAFICARD) [Chairman: B Sivaraman] set up by the RBI in its report submitted in 1979 recommended the establishment of NABARD. The Parliament through the Act 61 of 1981, approved its setting up.

CRAFICARD, after reviewing the then existing arrangements, came to the conclusion that a new arrangement would be necessary at the national level for achieving the desired focus and thrust towards integration of credit activities in the context of the strategy for Integrated Rural Development Programme (IRDP). Against the backdrop of the massive credit needs of rural development and the need to uplift the weaker sections in the rural areas within a given time horizon, the arrangement called for a separate institutional set up. Similarly, The Reserve Bank had onerous responsibilities to discharge in respect of its many basic functions of central banking in monetary and credit regulations and was not therefore in a position to devote undivided attention to the operational details of the emerging complex credit problems. This paved the way for the establishment of NABARD.

CRAFICARD also found it prudent to integrate short-term, medium-term and long-term credit structure for the agriculture sector by establishing a new bank. NABARD is the result of this recommendation. It was set up with an initial capital of ₹ 100 crore, which was enhanced to ₹ 2,000 crore, fully subscribed by the Government of India and the RBI.

6.3.2 Objectives: NABARD was established in terms of the Preamble to the Act, "for providing credit for the promotion of agriculture, small-scale industries, cottage and village industries, handicrafts and other rural crafts and other allied economic activities in rural areas with a view to promoting IRDP and securing prosperity of rural areas and for matters connected therewith in incidental thereto".

The main objectives of the NABARD as stated in the statement of objectives while placing the bill before the Lok Sabha were categorized as under:

1. The National Bank will be an apex organisation in respect of all matters relating to policy, planning operational aspects in the field of credit for promotion of agriculture, small scale industries, cottage and village industries, handicrafts and other rural crafts and other allied economic activities in rural areas.
2. The Bank will serve as a refinancing institution for institutional credit such as long-term, short-term for the promotion of activities in the rural areas.
3. The Bank will also provide direct lending to any institution as may be approved by the Central Government.
4. The Bank will have organic links with the Reserve Bank of India and maintain a close link within.

6.3.3 Major Activities: These are as under:

1. Preparing of potential linked credit plans for identification of

exploitable potentials under agriculture and other activities available for development through bank credit.

2. Refinancing banks for extending loans for investment and production purpose in rural areas.
3. Providing loans to State government/non-governmental organizations (NGOs)/panchayati raj institutions (PRIs) for developing rural infrastructure.
4. Supporting credit innovations of non-governmental organizations (NGOs) and other non-formal agencies.
5. Extending formal banking services to the unreached rural poor by evolving a supplementary credit delivery strategy in a cost effective manner by promoting self-help groups (SHGs).
6. Promoting participatory watershed development for enhancing productivity and profitability of rain-fed agriculture in a sustainable manner.
7. On-site inspection of cooperative banks and regional rural banks (RRBs) and off-site surveillance over health of cooperatives and RRBs.

6.3.4 Role and Functions: These are as under:

1. NABARD is an apex institution accredited with all matters concerning policy, planning and operations in the field of credit for agriculture and other economic activities in rural areas.
2. It is an apex refinancing agency for the institutions providing investment and production credit for promoting the various developmental activities in rural areas.
3. It takes measures towards institution building for improving absorptive capacity of the credit delivery system, including monitoring, formulation of rehabilitation schemes, restructuring of credit institutions, training of personnel etc.
4. It co-ordinates the rural financing activities of all the institutions engaged in developmental work at the field level and maintains liaison with Government of India, State Governments, Reserve Bank of India and other national level institutions concerned with policy formulation.

5. It prepares, on annual basis, rural credit plans for all districts in the country; these plans form the base for annual credit plans of all rural financial institutions.
6. It undertakes monitoring and evaluation of projects refinanced by it.
7. It promotes research in the fields of rural banking, agriculture and rural development.

6.3.5 Mission: It has the mission of promoting sustainable and equitable agriculture and rural development through effective credit support, related services, institution building and other innovative initiatives.

In pursuing this mission, NABARD focuses its activities on the following:

1. **Credit Functions**: These involve preparation of potential-linked credit plans annually for all districts of the country for identification of credit potential, monitoring the flow of ground level rural credit, issuing policy and operational guidelines to rural financing institutions and providing credit facilities to eligible institutions under various programmes.
2. **Development Functions**: These concern reinforcement of the credit functions and making credit more productive.
3. **Supervisory Functions**: These ensure the proper functioning of cooperative banks and regional rural banks.

6.3.6 Role in Training: Section 38 of the NABARD Act provides that the Bank shall:

1. Maintain expert staff to study all problems relating to agriculture and rural development and be available for consultation to the Central Government, the Reserve Bank of India, the State governments and the other institutions engaged in the field of rural development.
2. Provide facilities for training, for dissemination of information and the promotion of research including the undertaking of studies, researches, techno-economic and other surveys in the field of rural banking, agriculture and rural development.
3. Provide technical, legal, financial, marketing and

administrative assistance to any person engaged in agriculture and rural development activities.

4. Provide consultancy services in the field of agriculture and rural development and other related matters in or outside India, on such terms and against such remuneration, as may be agreed upon.

In this context, the role of training in NABARD and the role played by it for capacity building in client institutions, partner agencies and other developmental agencies is important.

In pursuance of the Bank's mandate as stated in the Act, the Bank provides training facilities for the RFIs and agencies involved in rural development through BIRD and the two RTCs. With a view to broad-base the training and capacity building efforts, the Bank encourages the RFIs to set up their own training systems and provides these training institutes the necessary support to conduct meaningful and quality training. Options and avenues for strengthening the training interventions at the client level are continuously examined so that the human resources in these institutions are developed to take on the challenges, reckon with the competition, improve customer service, expand outreach, develop suitable products and thereby contribute to rural development.

6.3.7 NABARD Consultancy Services (Nabcons): Nabcons is a wholly owned subsidiary promoted by NABARD and is engaged in providing consultancy in all spheres of agriculture, rural development and allied areas. Nabcons leverages on the core competence of the NABARD in the areas of agricultural and rural development, especially multidisciplinary projects, banking, institutional development, infrastructure, training etc., internalized for more than two decades.

In tune with NABARD's mission to bring about rural prosperity, Nabcons has more than just commercial interest in the assignments it undertakes.

6.3.8 Bankers Institute of Rural Development (BIRD): Established in 1983 at Lucknow, it is an autonomous institute promoted and funded by NABARD. BIRD was established primarily to cater to the training needs of RRB personnel. The Institute, has, since April 1, 1992, been catering to the training and information needs of rural bankers through its topical training programs/seminars. The Institute's mandate also includes research and consultancy in the related areas.

6.3.9 NABARD's Strategy for Popularity of Micro Finance: NABARD is adopting the following strategy to spread the outreach of SHG-Bank Linkage Programme.

1. Widening spatial distribution and intensity of the outreach of the Programme with district oriented planning and strategy.
2. Evolving district-wise plan of action/strategy in consultation with existing stakeholders aiming at promotion and linkage of a minimum of 500 SHGs per district every year.
3. Training and exposure programmes for the staff of the stakeholders.
4. Providing promotional assistance to partners for promoting and nurturing the SHGs generally on an *add-on* basis.
5. Widening the range of SHG promoting agencies.
6. Involving banks at their corporate level, organising training programmes for the regional/zonal managers of commercial banks in association with their central offices.
7. Establishing the financing of SHGs as a business proposition for banks.
8. Increasing the participation of the co-operative banks by encouraging them to finance SHGs as *financing cooperatives within the co-operatives*.
9. Associating village communities, people's institutions, rural volunteers and individuals to participate in the programme as SHG promoters.
10. Increasing the quality of the existing SHGs by propagating *self-rating* tools.
11. Large-scale dissemination of the concept and approach among the rural masses.
12. Encouraging the NGOs to play an important role in

correcting the regional imbalances in spread of SHG-Bank Linkage Programme.

6.3.10 Tracking the Progress of Micro Finance: In view of the large outreach and pre-dominant position of the micro finance programme, it is important to keep a continuous track of the status, progress, trends, qualitative and quantitative performance comprehensively. To achieve this objective, Reserve Bank of India and NABARD issued guidelines in the year 2006-07 to commercial banks, regional rural banks and co-operative banks to furnish data on progress under micro finance. The data so collected covers various parameters like savings of SHGs with banks, bank loan disbursed to SHGs, bank loan outstanding against SHGs, gross non-performing assets of bank loans to SHGs, recovery performance of loans to SHGs. Further, the banks also furnish the data regarding bank loans provided to micro finance institutions (MFIs). NABARD, has been bringing out the consolidated document annually.

The data furnished by the banks have been analysed on a region-wise, state-wise, agency-wise, bank-wise and also for SHGs exclusively under Swarnajayanti Gram Swarojgar Yojana and exclusive women SHGs.

The major support provided by NABARD under Micro Finance Development and Equity Fund relates to promotion and nurturing of SHGs by self-help promoting institutions and training and capacity building of the stakeholders in the sector. NABARD is also experimenting innovative projects for further developing the micro finance through Joint Liability Groups.

Since 2006-07, NABARD has been compiling and analysing the data on progress made in micro finance sector, based on the returns furnished by commercial banks (CBs), regional rural banks (RRBs) and cooperative banks operating in the country. Most of the banks participating in the process of microfinance have reported the progress made under the programme.

NABARD has been instrumental in facilitating various activities under micro finance sector, involving all possible partners at the ground level in the field. NABARD has been encouraging voluntary agencies, bankers, socially spirited individuals, other formal and informal entities and also government functionaries to promote and nurture SHGs. The focus in this direction has been on training and capacity building of partners, promotional grant assistance to self-help promoting institutions (SHPIs), revolving fund assistance (RFA) to MFIs, equity/capital support to MFIs to supplement their financial resources and provision of 100 percent refinance against bank loans provided by various banks for microfinance activities.

7

Kisan Credit Cards (KCCs)

KCC is a pioneering credit delivery innovation—launched by NABARD in August 1998—for providing adequate and timely credit to farmers under single window, with flexible and simplified procedure, adopting whole farm approach, including the short-term credit, medium term and long term credit needs of the borrowers for agriculture and allied activities and a reasonable component for consumption needs.

Beneficiaries covered under the scheme are issued with a credit card and a pass book or a credit card cum pass book incorporating the name, address, particulars of land holding, borrowing limit, validity period, a passport size photograph of holder etc., which may serve both as an identity card and facilitate recording of transactions on an ongoing basis. Borrower is required to produce the card-cum-pass book whenever he/she operates the account.

7.1 Objectives of the Scheme

These are as under:

1. To provide insurance coverage and financial support to the farmers in the event of failure of crops as a result of natural calamities, pests and diseases.
2. To encourage farmers to adopt progressive farming practices, high value inputs and higher technology in agriculture.
3. To help stabilise farm incomes, particularly in disaster years.
4. To support and stimulate primarily production of food crops and oilseeds.

7.2 Salient Features of the KCC Scheme

These are as follows:

1. Eligible farmers are provided with KCC and a pass book

or card-cum-pass book.

2. Revolving cash credit facility involving any number of drawals and repayments is allowed within the limit.
3. Limit is fixed on the basis of operational land holding, cropping pattern and scale of finance.
4. Entire production credit needs for full year plus ancillary activities related to crop production are considered while fixing limit.
5. Sub-limits to cover short-term, medium-term as well as term credit are fixed at the discretion of banks.
6. Card is valid for 3 to 5 years subject to annual review. As incentive for good performance, credit limits can be enhanced to take care of increase in costs, change in cropping pattern etc.
7. Each drawal is to be repaid within a maximum period of 12 months.
8. Conversion/re-schedulement of loans is permissible in case of damage to crops due to natural calamities.
9. Security, margin, rate of interest etc. are as per RBI norms.
10. Operations may be through issuing branch (and also PACS in the case of co-operative banks) through other designated branches at the discretion of bank.
11. Withdrawals through slips/cheques accompanied by card and passbook are allowed.
12. Crop loans disbursed under KCC scheme for notified crops are covered under Rashtriya Krishi Bima Yojna (National Crop Insurance Scheme)—a crop insurance scheme introduced at the behest of Government of India to protect the interest of the farmer against loss of crop yield caused by natural calamities, pest attacks etc.
13. All farmers (both loanee and non-loanee irrespective of their size of holdings) including sharecroppers, tenant farmers growing insurable crops covered.
14. The sum insured extends up to the value of threshold yield of the crop, with an option to cover up to 150 percent of average yield of the crop on payment of extra premium.

15. 50 percent subsidy in premium allowed to small and marginal farmers, to be shared equally by the Government of India and State Government/Union Territory. Premium subsidy to be phased out over a period of 5 years.

7.3 Advantages of the KCC Scheme to the Farmers

These include the following:

1. Access to adequate and timely credit to farmers.
2. Full year's credit requirement of the borrower taken care of.
3. Minimum paper work and simplification of documentation for drawal of funds from the bank.
4. Flexibility to draw cash at any time and buy inputs as per the need of the farmer and also to repay as and when surplus fund is available.
5. Assured availability of credit at any time enabling reduced interest burden for the farmer.
6. Sanction of the facility for 3 years subject to annual review and satisfactory operations and provision for enhancement.
7. Flexibility of drawals from a branch other than the issuing branch at the discretion of the bank.

7.4 Benefits of the Scheme to the Banks

These are as under:

1. Reduction in work load for branch staff by avoidance of repeat appraisal and processing of loan papers under KCC scheme.
2. Minimum paper work and simplification of documentation for drawal of funds from the bank.
3. Improvement in recycling of funds and better recovery of loans.
4. Reduction in transaction cost to the banks.
5. Better Banker-Client relationships.

7.5 Personal Accident Insurance Scheme

This scheme covers risk of KCC holders against death or permanent disability resulting from accidents caused by external, violent and visible means. The salient features of the scheme are as under:

1. Death due to accident (within 12 months of the accident) caused by outward, violent and visible means—₹ 50,000.
2. Permanent total disability—₹ 50,000.
3. Loss of two limbs or two eyes or one limb and one eye—₹ 50,000.
4. Loss of one limb or one eye—₹ 25,000.
5. Nominated office of insurance company to issue a Master Insurance Policy to each DCCB/RRB covering all its KCC holders.
6. Premium payable ₹ 15 for a 1 year policy while ₹ 45 for a 3-year policy.
7. Designated insurance company will nominate one office at district level to function as nodal office for co-ordinating implementation of personal accident insurance scheme for KCC holders in the district.
8. Insurance coverage available under Policy only from date of receipt of premium at insurance company.
9. Banks to ensure to incorporate name of nominee in Kisan Credit Card-cum-Pass Book.
10. Simplified claim settlement procedure evolved under Scheme whereby an Enquiry-cum-Verification Committee comprising Branch Manager of implementing bank, Lead Bank Officer and representative of insurance company to certify nature of accident causing disability/death and recommend settlement of insurance claims.

7.6 KCC Initiatives by the Government of India

These are as follows:

1. KCC holders have been covered under Personal Accident Insurance Scheme against accidental death or permanent disability, up to maximum amount of ₹ 50,000 and ₹ 25,000 respectively. The premium burden will be shared by the card issuing institutions and the borrower in the ratio of 2:1.

2. Bankers have also been advised to issue KCC to tenant farmers/share croppers/oral lessee/Joint liability groups.
3. Banks have been advised to cover all eligible farmers under KCC scheme.
4. With a view to make the scheme more effective at ground level and serve the farmers in the way in which it was expected to do, Government of India had constituted a High Level Task Force which shall inter alia examine and suggest measures for improving efficiency of KCC scheme. The report from task force was submitted to Government on June 30, 2010.

7.7 Major Steps Taken by NABARD

These are the following:

1. Co-operative banks and RRBs have been advised to enlarge the scope of the KCC scheme to cover term loans for agriculture and allied activities, including a reasonable component to meet the consumption needs, besides the existing facility of providing crop loan limit.
2. The coverage of KCC has been extended to landless labourers, oral lessees, tenant farmers including defaulters.
3. The concept of KCC has been extended to the borrowers of the long-term co-operative structure.
4. Studies on KCC Scheme have been conducted by NABARD periodically to facilitate feedback on the ground level issues/problems so that changes, where necessary, could be considered.
5. Commercial banks, co-operative banks and RRBs have been advised that they may, at their discretion, pay interest at a rate based on their perception and other relevant factors on the minimum credit balances in the cash credit accounts under the Kisan Credit Cards of farmers during the period from 10th to the last day of each calendar month.
6. RRBs have been advised to initiate innovative publicity campaign in each area of operation in order to cater all eligible farmers under KCC.

KCC scheme is in operation in all States and Union Territories (except Chandigarh, Daman and Diu and Dadra and Nagar Haveli) with all co-operative banks, RRBs and commercial banks participating in it.

7.8 RuPay ATM-cum-Debit Kisan Credit Cards (RKCCs)

Kisan Credit Cards (KCCs) was a pioneering credit delivery innovation—launched by NABARD in August 1998—for providing adequate and timely credit to farmers under single window, with flexible and simplified procedure, adopting whole farm approach, including the short-term credit, medium term and long term credit needs of the borrowers for agriculture and allied activities and a reasonable component for consumption needs. In tandem with the digitisation initiatives of Government of India, KCCs have now been converted to Rupay ATM-cum-Debit Kisan Credit Cards (RKCCs).

Beneficiaries covered under the scheme are issued with a credit card and a pass book or a credit card cum pass book incorporating the name, address, particulars of land holding, borrowing limit, validity period, a passport size photograph of holder etc., which may serve both as an identity card and facilitate recording of transactions on an ongoing basis. Borrower is required to produce the card-cum-pass book whenever he/she operates the account.

7.8.1 Objectives of the Scheme: These are as under:

1. To provide insurance coverage and financial support to the farmers in the event of failure of crops as a result of natural calamities, pests and diseases.
2. To encourage farmers to adopt progressive farming practices, high value inputs and higher technology in agriculture.
3. To help stabilise farm incomes, particularly in disaster years.
4. To support and stimulate primarily production of food crops and oilseeds.

7.8.2 Salient Features of the RKCC Scheme: These are as follows:

1. Eligible farmers are provided with RKCC and a pass book

or card-cum-pass book.

2. Revolving cash credit facility involving any number of drawals and repayments is allowed within the limit.
3. Limit is fixed on the basis of operational land holding, cropping pattern and scale of finance.
4. Entire production credit needs for full year plus ancillary activities related to crop production are considered while fixing limit.
5. Sub-limits to cover short-term, medium-term as well as term credit are fixed at the discretion of banks.
6. Card is valid for 3 to 5 years subject to annual review. As incentive for good performance, credit limits can be enhanced to take care of increase in costs, change in cropping pattern etc.
7. Each drawal is to be repaid within a maximum period of 12 months.
8. Conversion/re-schedulement of loans is permissible in case of damage to crops due to natural calamities.
9. Security, margin, rate of interest etc. are as per RBI norms.
10. Operations may be through issuing branch (and also PACS in the case of co-operative banks) through other designated branches at the discretion of bank.
11. Withdrawals through slips/cheques accompanied by card and passbook are allowed.
12. Crop loans disbursed under RKCC scheme for notified crops are covered under Rashtriya Krishi Bima Yojna (National Crop Insurance Scheme)—a crop insurance scheme introduced at the behest of Government of India to protect the interest of the farmer against loss of crop yield caused by natural calamities, pest attacks etc.
13. All farmers (both loanee and non-loanee irrespective of their size of holdings) including sharecroppers, tenant farmers growing insurable crops covered.
14. The sum insured extends up to the value of threshold yield of the crop, with an option to cover up to 150 percent of average yield of the crop on payment of extra premium.

7.8.3 Advantages of the RKCC Scheme to the Farmers: These include the following:

1. Access to adequate and timely credit to farmers.
2. Full year's credit requirement of the borrower taken care of.
3. Minimum paper work and simplification of documentation for drawal of funds from the bank.
4. Flexibility to draw cash at any time and buy inputs as per the need of the farmer and also to repay as and when surplus fund is available.
5. Assured availability of credit at any time enabling reduced interest burden for the farmer.
6. Sanction of the facility for 3 years subject to annual review and satisfactory operations and provision for enhancement.
7. Flexibility of drawals from a branch other than the issuing branch at the discretion of the bank.

7.8.4 Benefits of the Scheme to the Banks: These are as under:

1. Reduction in work load for branch staff by avoidance of repeat appraisal and processing of loan papers under RKCC scheme.
2. Minimum paper work and simplification of documentation for drawal of funds from the bank.
3. Improvement in recycling of funds and better recovery of loans.
4. Reduction in transaction cost to the banks.
5. Better Banker-Client relationships.

7.9 KCC Scheme: An Assessment

KCC scheme, introduced in 1998-99, aims at providing crop loans to farmers in a flexible and cost-effective manner. The scheme is being implemented in all the States and Union Territories by all commercial banks, RRBs, state co-operative banks, central co-operative banks, and primary agricultural co-operative societies. Beneficiaries covered under the KCC are issued with a credit card and a pass book or a credit card-cum-pass book incorporating the name, address and particulars of land, borrowing limit, and the validity period.

Production credit limits are fixed taking into account the entire production credit needs for a full year plus ancillary activities relating to crop production. Sub-limits are also fixed at the discretion of lending banks. Crop loan/short-term credit is in the form of a revolving cash credit facility involving any number of drawals and repayments within the limit fixed on the basis of operational land holding, cropping pattern and scale of finance.

At the instance of the RBI, the National Council of Applied Economic Research (NCAER) conducted a survey for assessing the impact of the KCC scheme. The survey brought out several advantages of the KCC scheme in terms of increase in the flow of credit to the agriculture sector, reduction in borrowings from the informal sector, significant savings in time spent on obtaining credit and an overall reduction in cost of credit delivery. The survey had identified areas requiring policy initiatives to make the scheme more effective. These relate to restrictions imposed on the issuance of KCCs by banks, restrictions on use of KCCs only at card issuing branches, non-availability of incentives for timely repayments, low credit limits and low awareness regarding the provision of personal accident insurance scheme. The RBI has advised the Indian Banks Association to examine these suggestions and come up with remedial measures.

KCC scheme has increased farmers' access to short term credit. The objective of the scheme is to provide adequate and timely support from the banking system to the farmers for their cultivation needs including purchases of inputs in a flexible and cost effective manner. Loans disbursed under KCCs are now covered under Rashtriya Krishi Beema Yojna of the General Insurance Corporation. KCC holders are being provided personal accident insurance cover of ₹ 50,000 for accidental death and ₹ 25,000 for permanent disability.

The introduction of KCCs was a significant innovation in the rural credit delivery mechanism. However, the outreach of the KCCs to cover all eligible farmers under the scheme has been hampered by the lack of updated land records, small landholdings and illiteracy of borrowers. The growing popularity of the KCC scheme reflects its effectiveness in ensuring hassle-free and timely operations as also availability of credit with minimum transaction cost and documentation.

To sum up, KCC scheme aims to provide an adequate and timely institutional credit to farmers with simplified and flexible procedures. The scheme is implemented by SCBs, RRBs, and co-operative banks. It comprises both short-term crop loan and term loan components.

8

Farm Loan Waivers

Rural indebtedness is noted as a major reason for the spurt in farmer suicides during recent times across a number of states. In most, if not all, such cases, the economic status of the suicide victim was very poor, being small and marginal farmers. After the Green Revolution agricultural activities have become cash-based individual enterprises requiring high investment in modern inputs and wage labour. This is evident from the list of states with high incidence of farmer suicides, which are not necessarily backward or predominantly agrarian or with low income. Increased liberalization and globalisation have in fact led to a shift in cropping pattern from staple crops to cash crops like oilseeds and cotton, requiring high investment in modern inputs and wage labour, and increasing credit needs but when the prices decline farmers have no means to supplement their incomes.

Farm loans may be crop loans or investment loans taken to buy equipment. Both farmers and banks reap a good harvest when all is well. However, when there is a poor monsoon or natural calamity, farmers may be unable to repay loans. The rural distress in such situations often prompts Centre/States to offer relief—reduction or complete waiver of loans.

Essentially, the Centre/States take over the liability of farmers and repay the banks. Waivers are usually selective, i.e. only certain loan types, categories of farmers or loan sources may qualify. For instance, in 2008 crop loans and investment loans were waived for marginal and small farmers (those with less than 2 hectares of land ownership). Other farmers were only given a 25 percent reduction.

8.1 Need for Loan Waivers

Agriculture in India has been facing many constraints like

fragmented land holding, depleting water table levels, deteriorating soil quality, rising input costs, low productivity etc. Add to this the vagaries of the monsoon. Output prices may not be remunerative. Farmers are often forced to borrow to manage expenses. Also, many small farmers not eligible for bank credit, borrow at exorbitant interest rates from private sources.

When nature rides roughshod over debt-ridden farmers in the form of erratic monsoon and crop failures, they face grim options. Indebtedness is a key reason for many suicides by farmers in the country. Loan waivers provide some relief to farmers in such situations. Farm loan waivers are not new in India and almost all major political parties are guilty of announcing them in a bid to further their performance at the hustings. In fact, the recent resurgence of farm loan waiver culture in the Indian polity has got many economists and policy makers worried.

In a country where bulk of the farm land is rain-fed, the need to offer some relief to a drought-hit farmer is real.

8.2 Agricultural Debt Waiver and Debt Relief Scheme, 2008

In the wake of suicides by farmers in some parts of the country, indebtedness of the farmers was high on the agenda of the Government. The Government had appointed a Committee (Chairman: R. Radhakrishna) to examine all aspects of agricultural indebtedness. The Committee in its report made a number of recommendations but stopped short of recommending waiver of agricultural loans. However, Government was conscious of the problems being faced by the farmers, especially the small and marginal farmers. Having carefully weighed the pros and cons of debt waiver and having taken into account the resource position, Finance Minister P. Chidambaram announced on February 29, 2008, a relief package for farmers which included the complete waiver of loans given to small and marginal farmers. The Finance Minister announced the following scheme of debt waiver and debt relief for farmers:

1. All agricultural loans disbursed by scheduled commercial

banks, regional rural banks and co-operative credit institutions up to March 31, 2007 and overdue as on December 31, 2007 were covered under the scheme.

2. For marginal farmers (i.e., holding up to 1 hectare) and small farmers (1-2 hectare), there was a complete waiver of all loans that were overdue on December 31, 2007 and which remained unpaid until February 29, 2008. In respect of other farmers, there was a one time settlement (OTS) scheme for all loans that were overdue on December 31, 2007 and which remained unpaid until February 29, 2008. Under the OTS, a rebate of 25 percent was given against payment of the balance of 75 percent.
3. Agricultural loans were restructured and rescheduled by banks in 2004 and 2006 through special packages. These rescheduled loans, and other loans rescheduled in the normal course as per RBI guidelines, were also eligible either for a waiver or an OTS on the same pattern.
4. The implementation of the debt waiver and debt relief scheme was to be completed by June 30, 2008. Upon being granted debt waiver or signing an agreement for debt relief under the OTS, the farmer was entitled to fresh agricultural loans from the banks in accordance with normal rules.
5. Government estimated that about 3 crore small and marginal farmers and about 1 crore other farmers would benefit from the scheme. The total value of overdue loans waived was estimated at ₹ 50,000 crore and the OTS relief on the overdue loans at ₹ 10,000 crore.

In addition to above, the government initiated several measures to galvanize the institutional credit system to make it more responsive to the needs of farmers. Some of the important measures initiated in this regard were as under:

1. Banks were advised to simplify rules and procedures for documentation for agricultural loans.
2. As part of the measures announced by the RBI for financial inclusion, banks were advised to open *no frills*

accounts and issue simpie overdraft facility against such accounts. Banks were also advised to issue general credit cards up to ₹ 25,000 without insisting on security and end use of funds.

3. Banks were advised to undertake, on a pilot basis, 100 percent financial inclusion in at least one district in each State. Based on the success of the pilot, the State Level Bankers Committee in the States would draw a time-bound plan for achieving 100 percent financial inclusion in other districts of the State.

8.3 Flipside of Farm Loan Waivers

There are debates about the long-term effectiveness of such relief measures. In fact, several drawbacks have been pointed out with respect to loan waivers:

1. It is said that farm loan waivers are at best a temporary solution and entail a moral hazard—even those who can afford to pay may not pay, in the expectation of a waiver.
2. Such measures can erode credit discipline and may make banks wary of lending to farmers in the future. Farm loan waivers can discourage subsequent lending by banks in districts with greater exposure to the debt waiver, harming farmers over the long-run.
3. Loan waivers make a sharp dent in the finances of the governments. A higher fiscal deficit is typically funded through borrowings. When government borrowing increases, it crowds out the private sector and causes interest rates to rise which act as a stumbling block for a faster pace of economic growth.
4. Waivers may add to the already elevated non-performing assets of banks.
5. In many cases, one household has multiple loans either from different sources or in the name of different family members, which entitles it to multiple loan waiving.
6. Loan waiving excludes agricultural labourers who are even weaker than cultivators in bearing the consequences of

economic distress.

7. It severely erodes the credit culture, with dire long-run consequences to the banking business.
8. Loan waiving is prone to serious exclusion and inclusion errors, as evidenced by the Comptroller and Auditor General's (CAG) findings in the Agricultural Debt Waiver and Debt Relief Scheme, 2008. They suggested that a more inclusive alternative approach is to identify the vulnerable farmers' based on certain criteria and give an equal amount as financial relief to the vulnerable and distressed families.
9. Loan waivers cover only formal sources of credit and exclude any kind of informal loan. Thus, while it benefits wealthy and large-scale farmers who have access to institutional credit, small and marginal farmers, who borrow the majority of their funds from private moneylenders, do not benefit from such reliefs.

Opponents of loan waivers demand making agriculture sustainable by reducing inefficiencies, increasing income, reducing costs and providing protection through insurance schemes. A better long-term solution would be to invest in weather proofing Indian agriculture. Building irrigation infrastructure, connecting rivers, adopting dry land farming, changing cropping patterns and embracing modern/more efficient farming practices will help. Also, promoting crop insurance will prove to be useful and if required, the government can subsidise the premium to make such insurance schemes attractive for both insurers and farmers.

However, farmers can decide the fortunes of political parties, and politicians are wary of antagonising them. Former RBI governor Urjit Patel was right in calling for a consensus among political parties against announcing this populist but economically debilitating measure.

Part III
Agricultural Marketing and Commerce

9

Importance and Requirements of a Sound Agricultural Marketing System

Disposal of the produce after harvest and the return obtained have a significant effect on production and on the welfare of the cultivator.

9.1 Nature and Significance of Agricultural Marketing

Marketing is the last link in the chain of production process. An efficient marketing system which ensures reasonable return to the producers is essential to induce them to produce more. Production in agriculture being seasonal, the crop is harvested during a short period and consumed gradually. While commodities like cotton and groundnut require large storage space which the average cultivator lacks, fruits, vegetables and sugarcane are of a perishable nature. The farmer has, therefore, to dispose of his surplus immediately either at the village or at the *mandi.* In the absence of staying power of a large number of small farmers, they compete with each other and the markets witness conditions of occasional glut and scarcity. A major part of the commercial crops like cotton, jute, sugarcane and oilseeds has to be marketed immediately as the farmers are in need of cash for meeting their dues and other expenses. As regards foodgrains the marketable surplus varies by crops and regions. The total quantity and value of the marketed produce, even in a predominantly subsistence economy as in India is considerable.

Sale of agricultural produce involves a number of functions such as assembling, storing, grading, standardising, transporting and financing the produce and negotiating sale. Some of these operations may be performed by the farmer, but storage and sale of a commodity and finding finance for purchase, call for specialised knowledge and adequate resources which the individual cultivator does not possess.

The village money lender or the *mandi arhatiya* advances loans to farmers for securing production requirements like seeds, and manures and for meeting other needs. These debts some times carry an understanding or an obligation to sell the produce to or through the lender or his nominee. At the time of sale the position of advantage occupied by the village banker gets reflected either in a lower price or unfair weights or delayed settlement. If the sale takes place in the *mandi* or the market through the brokers or *arhatiyas* the farmer pays not only for the services rendered by the middlemen but is also subjected to other unwarranted deductions.

The benefits of a regulated market which attempt only to improve the existing practices are limited. Without changing the marketing structure the number of middlemen and costs cannot be reduced. Efforts in this direction have been made in some States by organising cooperative marketing. The progress of marketing societies, in spite of immense scope, has so far been slow. The entry of a co-operative even as an agent is not generally favoured by the trade.

9.2 Requirements for a Sound Agricultural Marketing System

Defects in the present system of agricultural marketing can be removed by providing the following facilities to the farmers:

1. In view of the poverty of the Indian farmers, it is necessary to provide them with credit facilities at the time of harvest so that they are not forced to sell their produce at that time. Soon after the harvest, the prices of agricultural products are relatively low. Farmers should have the choice to wait for better times, i.e. better prices. This can be done by providing them with short-term credit to build their staying power.
2. If the farmers decide to postpone the sale of their produce in view of low prices at the time of harvest, they should have proper warehousing facilities. Government should provide scientific storage facilities at reasonable charges in or near the villages. This task can be entrusted to the Central

Warehousing Corporation and the State Warehousing Corporations.

3. Next in logical order are the transport facilities. Villages in India are not well connected with cities and townships through *pucca* roads or railways. If efficient transport facilities are available to farmers throughout the year, they can take their produce to markets of their choice to secure remunerative prices.
4. It is also necessary to provide adequate and latest information to the farmers regarding prices of various agricultural commodities prevailing in different markets. Although this is being done through radio and television, there is the need to extend the coverage of these facilities to all parts of the country.
5. Farmers should be provided with reasonable amenities in the *mandies*. Efforts should be made to reduce the presence of large number of middlemen in the *mandies* who erode profits of the farmers considerably. Arrangements should exist for grading and standardisation of agricultural produce. Moreover, provision should be made for following facilities in the *mandies,* viz. post office, banking, lodging and boarding for overnight stay and parking for vehicles.

Improvement in the marketing system will go a long way to ensure remunerative prices to the farmers, inducing them to produce more.

9.3 Inter-Ministerial Task Force on Agricultural Marketing

The Inter-Ministerial Task Force set up by the Ministry of Agriculture to strengthen and develop agricultural marketing submitted its Report in June 2002, outlining several reforms in agricultural marketing. It recommended amendment to the States' Agricultural Produce Marketing Acts for promotion of direct marketing and contract farming, development of agricultural markets in private and cooperative sectors, stepping up of pledge financing, expansion of futures trading to cover all agricultural commodities, introduction of negotiable warehousing receipt system and use of information technology to provide market led extension services to farmers. At a National Conference on Agriculture Marketing Reforms organized by the Ministry of Agriculture on September 27, 2002 in New Delhi, all the State Governments and Union Territory Administrations were requested to implement the reforms measures by bringing out suitable amendments in the existing state legislation. A Committee of State Ministers was also set up under the Chairmanship of Union Minister of State (Agriculture) to accelerate the implementation of the reform measures.

9.4 Tenth Five Year Plan (2002-07) on Agricultural Marketing

Tenth Plan recommended the following combination of policy reforms which it thought would benefit both farmers and food consumers:

Single Market:

1. Amend the Essential Commodities Act to make it an emergency provision that will have to be formally invoked by a notification for a limited period.
2. Enact a Central Act to ban controls on movement within and between States.
3. Abolish octroi and all sorts of taxes/levies on food articles.

Competitive Grain Procurement:

1. Phase out all forms of monopoly purchase.
2. State Food Corporations should be allowed and encouraged to operate in all States.
3. Role of private agencies in food procurement activities should be gradually enhanced.

De-licensing:

1. Remove licensing controls and de-reserve all agro-based and food processing industries in a time-bound manner.
2. Phase out controls on sugar and its by-products and also remove sugar from the PDS.
3. Remove the present restrictions on establishing new milk processing capacity under the Milk and Milk Products Order.

4. De-reserve roller flour mills.
5. Remove rapeseed and groundnut processing units from the small-scale industries (SSI) list.
6. De-reserve all pesticides and fungicides.
7. De-license and de-control fertiliser production.

Export De-control:

1. Announce a policy renouncing the use of export restrictions on agricultural commodities. Domestic shortages should be met by imports, not by imposing export controls. Remove all restrictions (e.g. canalisation) on the export of agro-products.
2. Lift the ban on futures trading and stocking of all agricultural commodities, and on institutional credit and finance for such activities.
3. Amend the Agricultural Produce Marketing Acts of states to allow direct purchase of grain and other produce from farmers by agro-produce trading, storage and processing companies.
4. Support and promote provision of all types of insurance (health and hospitalisation, crop and weather) to farmers and other rural inhabitants. Give income tax incentives to insurance companies for a specified promotional period (five years). Allow 100 percent foreign direct investment (FDI) in insurance for agriculture and rural areas.
5. Modernise the information and extension system for farmers.
6. Overhaul the agricultural research and development system so as to replace the bureaucratic, financial and administrative system with a modern system of professional management and accountability under the Societies Act and provide for academic autonomy and peer review.
7. Remove all central and state taxes on production and marketing of cereals and other food products.
8. Allow 26 percent FDI in food retailing. Food retailers would also be free to sell other agro-based and rural industrial products.

These reforms would set the stage for large-scale entry of

the private sector into agricultural procurement.

9.5 Eleventh Five Year Plan (2007-12) on Agricultural Marketing

Expressing concern about the unsatisfactory state of markets for agricultural produce, the Eleventh Plan Document remarked, "The markets lack even basic infrastructure at many places. When the APMCs, were first initiated there was significant gain in market infrastructure development. However, this infrastructure is now out of date, especially given the needs of a diversified agriculture. At present only one-fourth of the markets have common drying yards, trader modules viz. shop, godown, and platform in front of shop exist in only 63 percent of the markets. Cold storage units are needed in the markets where perishable commodities are brought for sale But exist only in 9 percent of the markets at present and grading facilities exist in less than one-third of the markets. The basic facilities viz. internal roads, boundary walls, electric lights, loading and unloading facilities and weighing equipment are available in more than 80 percent of the markets. Farmers' rest houses exist in more than half of the regulated markets. Covered or open auction platforms exist in only 2/3rd of regulated markets. It is evident from the above that there is considerable gap in the facilities available in the market yards. Also the farmers have to deal with non-transparent methods of price discovery and there is often lack of auction of graded items. Some modern markets will electronic auctioning have been introduced, but they are the exception. A major modernisation of this aspect of the infrastructure is urgently needed". [1]

9.6 Agricultural Marketing and Trade in the National Policy for Farmers, 2007

The National Policy for Farmers announced by the Government in 2007 envisaged various measures to improve marketing and trade practices related to agricultural produce. It observed, "Assured and remunerative marketing opportunities hold the key to continued progress in enhancing farm productivity and profitability. Several significant market reforms have already been initiated by the Central and the State governments. These reforms provide more options to farmers for selling their produce, allowing the private sector, including cooperatives, to develop markets, promote direct sales to consumers, processors and retail chain suppliers/exporters and remove scope for corruption and harassment. The following steps would be taken:

1. The Minimum Support Price (MSP) mechanism would be implemented effectively across the country.
2. The Market Intervention Scheme (MIS) would be strengthened to respond speedily to exigencies especially in the case of sensitive crops in the rain-fed areas.
3. The establishment of community foodgrains banks would be promoted to help in the marketing of underutilised crops and thereby generate an economic stake in the conservation of agro-biodiversity.
4. The food security basket will be enlarged by storing and selling nutritious millets such as bajra, jowar and ragi and other crops through the network of the Public Distribution System (PDS).
5. Efforts will be made to develop a single national market by relaxing internal restrictions. All controls and regulations hindering increase in farmers' income will be reviewed and abolished.
6. Terminal markets for agriculture would be developed in public-private partnership mode to provide better market access to farmers with better price realisation in a transparent trading environment with suitable backward linkages to give technical backstopping services needed for quality and demand driven production.
7. Role of the Agriculture Produce Market Committees and State Agriculture Marketing Boards would be transformed from mere regulatory focus to promotion of grading, branding, packaging and development of markets for local produce.

Farmers require authentic advice based on meteorological, marketing and management information for land-use decisions and investments. Infrastructure support would be put in place to minimise post-harvest losses and enable agro-processing and value-addition at the village level itself to increase employment and income. Farmers' organisations and other entities like cooperatives and small farmers' estates would be encouraged so that farmers can get a fair deal and enjoy the economies of scale. Producer groups and cooperatives will be encouraged to promote agro-processing industry. Constraints would be removed for improving the negotiability of warehouse receipts.

The trade policies in agriculture would aim at protecting the livelihood of farmer families and fostering their economic well-being. Effective livelihood security for farmers would be put in place. Quality and trade literacy programmes would be launched across the country. Appropriate measures would be introduced to mitigate price risks and enable the stakeholders, particularly the farmers, to hedge their risk.

Farmers' associations and SHGs would be supported to export on competitive terms by spreading awareness of the opportunities available for external agricultural trade and for value addition. The agri-export zones would be further strengthened to become places where farmers will get the best possible price for their produce.

The twin goals of ensuring justice to farmers in terms of a remunerative price for their produce and to consumers in terms of a fair and affordable price for staples (as farmers are also consumers) would be achieved through the following integrated strategy:

1. The government, while taking decisions on MSP, would ensure that the farmers' interests in receiving remunerative prices for their produce are adequately safeguarded.
2. Stable and efficient market environment, including effective implementation of MSP in rain-fed areas, would add to the improvement in productivity and income in dry land farming.

Terms of reference and status of the Commission for Agricultural Costs and Prices (CACP) would be reviewed to make the MSP regime more effective". [2]

9.7 Gramin Bhandaran Yojana (Rural Godown Scheme), 2007-12

It is well known that the small farmers do not have the economic strength to retain the produce with them till the market prices are favourable. There has been a felt need in the country to provide the farming community with facilities for scientific storage so that wastage and produce deterioration are avoided and also to enable it to meet its credit requirement without being compelled to sell the produce at a time when the prices are low. A network of rural godowns will enable small farmers to enhance their holding capacity in order to sell their produce at remunerative prices and avoid distress sales.

Accordingly, Grameen Bhandaran Yojana, a Capital Investment Subsidy Scheme for Construction/Renovation of Rural Godowns was introduced in 2001-02 and extended up to March 31, 2007. The scheme was extended for implementation during the period of the Eleventh Five Year Plan (2007-12), with modifications in its operational guidelines for new projects to be sanctioned after June 26, 2008.

9.7.1 Objectives of the Scheme: The main objectives of the scheme included the following:

1. Creation of scientific storage capacity with allied facilities in rural areas to meet the requirements of farmers for storing farm produce, processed farm produce and agricultural inputs.
2. Promotion of grading, standardization and quality control of agricultural produce to improve their marketability.
3. Prevention of distress sale immediately after harvest by providing the facility of pledge financing and marketing credit.
4. Strengthen agricultural marketing infrastructure in the country by paving the way for the introduction of a

national system of warehouse receipts in respect of agricultural commodities stored in such godowns.

5. To reverse the declining trend of investment in agriculture sector by encouraging private and cooperative sectors to invest in the creation of storage infrastructure in the country.

9.7.2 Salient Features of the Scheme: These were the following:

1. Projects for construction of rural godowns could be taken up by individuals, farmers, group of farmers, partnership firms, non-government organizations (NGOs), self-help groups (SHGs), companies, corporations, co-operatives, local bodies other than municipal corporations, federations, agricultural produce marketing committees, marketing boards and agro-processing corporations in the entire country. Assistance for renovation of rural godowns was restricted to godowns constructed by co-operatives only.
2. Under the scheme, the entrepreneur was free to construct godown at any place, as per his/her commercial judgment except for the restriction that it would be outside the limits of municipal corporation area. Rural godowns constructed in the food parks promoted by the Ministry of Food Processing Industries were also eligible under the scheme for assistance.
3. Capacity of a godown was decided by the entrepreneur. However, subsidy under the scheme was restricted to a minimum capacity of 100 tonnes and maximum capacity of 10,000 tonnes. There was no maximum ceiling on subsidy in the case of projects of rural godowns of co-operatives assisted by NCDC.
4. Rural godowns of smaller sizes up to 50 tonnes capacity were also eligible for subsidy under the scheme as a special case based on viability analysis depending on the topography/special requirement of the state/region. In hilly areas (where the project site was located at a height of more than 1,000 meters above mean sea level), rural

godowns of smaller size up to 25 tonnes capacity were also eligible for subsidy.

Endnotes

1. Government of India, Planning Commission, *Eleventh Five Year Plan* (2007-12), Volume III. p. 22.
2. Government of India, Ministry of Agriculture, Department of Agriculture and Co-operation, *National Policy for Farmers*, 2007, pp. 16-17.

10

Present System of Agricultural Marketing

During the pre-Independence period, Indian agriculture was backward and stagnant and there was hardly any marketable surplus. Therefore, the system of marketing, though defective, did not attract much attention. However, in the post-Independence period and particularly after the green revolution, agricultural marketing has become a prime concern for the planners. Due to increase in agricultural productivity, the marketable surplus has increased, necessitating reforms in the existing system. The objectives of these reforms are to ensure: (a) fair prices for the produce of the farmers, (b) adequate and regular availability of foodgrains for urban areas and (c) regular supplies of raw materials for the industries.

10.1 Various Systems of Agricultural Marketing

Presently, agricultural marketing is done through a variety of systems. An important traditional system is the sale of produce to money lenders and village traders. This system is closely related to the problem of rural indebtedness. Farmers who are indebted to moneylenders are forced to sell their produce to them. It is understandable that the price paid by the moneylenders is considerably lower than the market price.

Another traditional practice is the sale of produce in the *haats* and *shandies*. *Haats* are village markets held once or twice a week and serve a small cluster of villages. *Shandies* are also village markets held at longer intervals or on special occasions.

An important component of the marketing system is the widespread network of regulated wholesale markets. These markets are generally located near or in a township and serve a number of surrounding villages. The farmers sell their produce to the commission agents with the help of brokers. It is well-known that various types of malpractices exist in these markets, e.g. use of wrong measures and weights. *Haats* and *shandies* constitute, for a great majority of farmers in India, particularly the small producers, the focal points for disposal of farm produce as well as sale and purchase centres for non-agricultural products.

According to *Economic Survey, 2021-22*, "Wholesale agricultural marketing is undertaken by the network of 6,946 regulated wholesale markets, set up under the provision of respective State Agricultural Produce Market Committee (APMC) Act. Government of India has been working continuously and has taken several concrete steps to link the farmers with markets in order to help the farmers in trading and realising competitive and remunerative prices for their produce. For example, APMCs, have been recognized as one of the eligible entities under Agriculture Infrastructure Fund (AIF) to further strengthen the infrastructure in APMC mandis. All loans under the AIF have interest subvention of 3 percent per annum up to a limit of ₹ 2 crore. This subvention is available for a maximum period of 7 years. APMCs are eligible for multiple projects (of different infrastructure types) within their designated market area. In such cases, interest subvention for a loan up to ₹ 2 crore will be provided for each project of different infrastructure types, e.g. cold storage, sorting, grading and assaying units, silos etc. within the designated market area of the APMC". [1].

Involvement of government agencies with the marketing of agricultural produce is a welcome development. Co-operative societies and government agencies have helped the farmers to escape the exploitative practices of the private dealers. Leading agencies involved in procurement and support price operations on behalf of the Government are: Food Corporation of India, Cotton Corporation of India, Jute Corporation of India and the Co-operatives with National Agricultural Co-operative Marketing Federation (NAFED) as their apex organisation.

From time to time, government announces procurement or minimum support prices for various agricultural crops.

10.2 Marketing Organizations of the Government

The Government has been playing an important role in developing the agricultural marketing system in the country. The Ministry of Agriculture and Farmers Welfare has 3 organizations dealing with marketing under its administrative control, namely Directorate of Marketing and Inspection (DMI) Faridabad, Chaudhary Charan Singh National Institute of Agricultural Marketing (NIAM), Jaipur and Small Farmers Agri-business Consortium (SFAC), New Delhi.

10.2.1 Directorate of Marketing and Inspection (DMI): DMI is an attached office of the Ministry of Agriculture. It was set up in 1935 to implement the agricultural marketing policies and programmes of the Central Government. Since its inception, the Directorate continues to be responsible for bringing about an integrated development of marketing of agricultural and allied produce in the country with a view to safeguarding the interests of producer-sellers as well as the consumers. It maintains a close liaison between the Central and the State Governments in the implementation of agricultural marketing policies in the country.

A. Functions: The main functions of the DMI are the following:

1. Promotion of standardization and grading of agricultural and allied produce under the Agricultural Produce (Grading and Marking) Act, 1937 as amended in 1986.
2. Training of personnel in agricultural marketing.
3. Advising State Governments on regulation and management of agricultural produce markets.
4. Marketing extension.
5. Agricultural marketing information network.
6. Construction of rural godowns.
7. Development/strengthening of agricultural marketing infrastructure, grading and standardization.

B. Activities: The activities of the DMI cover the

following areas of agricultural marketing:

(a) Standardization and Grading: The Agricultural Produce (Grading and Marking) Act, 1937 provides for grading and marking of agricultural and other produce. The Act empowers the Central Government to make Rules for: (a) fixing grade designation to indicate quality of any scheduled article, (b) defining the quality indicated by every grade designation and (c) specifying grade designation marks to represent particular grade designations.

Standards notified as per the provisions of the Act are popularly called AGMARK Standards. These standards differentiate between quality and 2-3 grades are prescribed for each commodity. Grades help farmers/traders to get prices for agricultural commodities as per the quality produced by them and consumers get the desired quality.

Till date, grade standards for 203 agricultural commodities have been notified. These include fruits and vegetables, cereals, pulses, oilseeds, vegetable oils, ghee, spices, honey, creamery butter, wheat atta, besan etc.

These commodities can also be certified under AGMARK as per the prescribed grade standards. Vegetable oils, spices, ghee, creamery butter, honey, wheat atta, besan etc. are popularly certified under AGMARK. Grading and marking of agricultural commodities is voluntary as per the provisions of the Act.

(b) Regulation, Development and Management of Agricultural Produce Markets: Agricultural markets are regulated and managed under the Agricultural Produce Marketing (Regulation) Acts enacted by the respective State Governments. The Central Government provides guidance and assistance in regulation and development of agricultural produce markets. By the end of March 2010, 7,157 markets were brought under the ambit of regulation. In the perspective of agricultural marketing reforms, DMI prepared the Model APMC Act, 2003 and the Model APMC Rules, 2007 and circulated them to all the State Governments/UT Administrations for consideration and adoption.

(c) Construction of Rural Godowns: A network of rural godowns enables small farmers to avoid distress sale by enhancing their holding capacity and sell their produce at remunerative prices. Accordingly, DMI launched Grameen Bhandaran Yojana w.e.f. April 1, 2001. The main objectives of the scheme include creation of scientific storage capacity with allied facilities in rural areas to meet various requirements of farmers for storing farm produce, processed farm produce, agricultural inputs etc. and help them to avoid distress sale by creating the facility of pledge loan and marketing credit.

(d) Marketing Reforms: The State Governments have been advised suitably to modify APMC Act to facilitate: (a) development of competitive markets in private and cooperative sectors, (b) allow procurement of agricultural commodities directly from farmers fields and (c) to establish effective linkage between the farm production and the retail chain and food processing industries. In the wake of the economic liberalization, the concept of contract farming in which national and multi-national companies enter into contracts for marketing of agricultural produce and to provide technology and capital to farmers has gained importance. These arrangements have to be promoted as an effective method of linking small farmers to sources of extension, advice, mechanization, seeds and credit and to assured and profitable markets.

(e) Modern Terminal Market Complex: In order to harness the potential of emerging consumer demand for horticulture commodities, a professionally managed competitive alternate marketing structure which provides multiple choices to farmers for sale along with a comprehensive solution to meet key needs of the stakeholders is necessary. Such a system entails high investment cost and development of efficient skills, each of which can be infused by inviting private sector participation in the sector. Thus, the Modern Terminal Market in hub and spoke model was conceptualized to be set up on a public-private-partnership basis with the objective of fulfilling the above goals.

The scheme is being implemented through a subsidy route

under National Horticulture Mission with active involvement of all stakeholders at various levels under public-private-partnership mode.

10.2.2 Chaudhary Charan Singh National Institute of Agricultural Marketing (NIAM): NIAM is a premier national level institute set up by the Government of India in August 1988 to offer specialized training, research, education and consultancy in the field of agricultural marketing. NIAM is an autonomous body under the aegis of the Ministry of Agriculture, Government of India. It was set up as a Registered Society to cater to the needs of agricultural marketing personnel in India as well as from South East Asian Countries.

NIAM offers a two year Post-graduate Diploma in Agri-Business Management Programme (PGDABM) which is an AICTE approved residential programme, for students with undergraduate degree in Agriculture and Allied Sciences. The programme combines the best of MBA with unique skills required for a career in agri-business.

10.2.3 Small Farmers' Agri-Business Consortium (SFAC): SFAC was registered by Ministry of Agriculture, Government of India on January 18, 1994 as a society under the Societies Registration Act, 1860. Currently, the members include RBI, SBI, IDBI, EXIM Bank, Oriental Bank of Commerce, NABARD, Canara Bank, NAFED, United Phosphorous Ltd. etc. The mission of the society is to support innovative ideas for generating income and employment in rural areas by promoting private investment in agri-business projects.

The Central sector scheme for agri-business development is being implemented by SFAC in close association with commercial banks for providing:

1. Venture capital to agri-business projects.
2. Assistance to farmers/producers' groups for preparing quality Detailed Project Reports (DPR).

For effective implementation of the scheme, SFAC has already signed MoU with 21 commercial banks.

10.3 Agricultural Marketing Information Network (AGMARKNET), 2000

Market information is needed by farmers in planning production and marketing, and equally needed by other market participants in arriving at optimal trading decisions. The existence and dissemination of complete and accurate marketing information is the key to achieve both operational and pricing efficiency in the marketing system. Advancement in information and communication technology (ICT) has made the world a smaller place, and a larger market at one go. To fully utilize the new emerging trade opportunities for the benefit of farming community, there is a felt need to establish an ICT-based Agricultural Marketing Information Network in the country.

Towards this end, Ministry of Agriculture, Government of India launched the ICT-based Central sector scheme of AGMARKNET in March 2000 to link important agricultural produce markets spread all over the country and the State Agriculture Marketing Boards and Directorates. The project was executed with the technical support of National Informatics Centre (NIC). In order to facilitate wider market access to farm produce and better price discovery through value addition, the scheme is additionally disseminating information on market requirements in terms of quality, packing, standards, sanitary and phyto-sanitary conditions etc.

10.3.1 Objectives of the Scheme: These are the following:

1. To establish a nation-wide information network for speedy collection and dissemination of market information and data for its efficient and timely utilization.
2. To facilitate collection and dissemination of information related to better price realization by the farmers. This would cover:

- Market-related information such as market fee, market charges, costs, method of sale, payment, weighment, handling, market functionaries, development programmes, market laws, dispute settlement mechanism, composition of market committees, income and expenditure etc.

- Price-related information such as minimum, maximum and modal prices of varieties and qualities transacted, total arrivals and dispatches with destination, marketing costs and margins etc.
- Infrastructure-related information comprising facilities and services available to the farmers with regard to storage and warehousing, cold storage, direct marketing, contract farming, buy-back arrangements, grading, re-handling and repacking etc.
- Promotion-related information covering accepted standards and grades, labelling, sanitary and phyto-sanitary requirements, pledge finance, marketing credit and new opportunities available in respect of better marketing.

3. To sensitize and orient farmers to respond to new challenges in agricultural marketing by using ICT as a vehicle of extension.
4. To improve efficiency in agricultural marketing through regular training and extension for reaching region-specific farmers in their own language.
5. To provide assistance for marketing research to generate marketing information for its dissemination to farmers and other marketing functionaries at grass-root level to create an ambience of good marketing practices in the country.

The scheme continued during the Eleventh Five Year Plan (2007-12) by enhancing its scope to cover 500 additional markets including remaining principal regulated markets, if any, farmer/consumer markets, private markets, panchayat markets, urban markets and special commodity markets.

Following activities were proposed to be undertaken while implementing the scheme during the Plan period:

1. Information regarding export documentation, export infrastructure, transportation facilities, exporters, marketing experts, agri-business corporate, quality standards, grading

and packhouse infrastructure, plant quarantine facilities, package of best marketing practices, seasonality of commodities.

2. Information on contract farming, direct marketing opportunities, value addition facilities etc. to be enriched and tie-ups between farmers/growers and sponsors/buyers will be facilitated through the portal by evolving a specific software system through outsourcing of work to an expert agency.
3. Information on warehouses along with addresses, accreditation facilities and their distance, pledge financing facilities etc.
4. Development of a data validation software to identify the wrong reporting and for removal of undesirable data from the central data base.
5. Provision of electronic display boards at every networked market for displaying minimum and maximum price of important commodities, arrivals, temperature etc.
6. Translation of contents of portal into regional languages.
7. Strategic alliances with corporate, telecom players and private users for strengthening market intelligence services.

10.4 State Level Agricultural Produce Market Committee (APMC) Acts

Presently, markets in agricultural products are regulated under the Agricultural Produce Market Committee (APMC) Act enacted by State Governments. There are about 2,477 principal regulated markets and 4,843 sub-market yards. Effectively, India has thousands of agricultural markets. This Act notifies agricultural commodities produced in the region such as cereals, pulses, edible oilseed, fruits and vegetables and even chicken, goat, sheep, sugar, fish etc., and provides that first sale in these commodities can be conducted only under the aegis of the APMC through the commission agents licensed by the APMCs set up under the Act. The typical amenities available in or around the APMCs are: auction halls, weigh bridges, godowns, shops for retailers, canteens, roads, lights, drinking water, police station, post-office, borewells, warehouse, farmers amenity centre, tanks, water treatment plant, soil-testing laboratory, toilet blocks, etc. Various taxes, fees/charges and cess levied on the trades conducted in the markets are also notified under the Act.

10.4.1 Faulty Functioning of APMCs: There is a magnitudes and multiplicity of fees arising from the operation of the APMCs. They charge a market fee of buyers, and they charge a licensing fee from the commissioning agents who mediate between buyers and farmers. They also charge small licensing fees from a whole range of functionaries (warehousing agents, loading agents etc.). In addition, commissioning agents charge commission fees on transactions between buyers and farmers.

The levies and other market charges imposed by states vary widely. Statutory levics/mandi tax, VAT etc. are a major source of market distortion. Such high level of taxes at the first level of trading have significant cascading effects on the prices as the commodity passes through the supply chain.

Even the model APMC Act treats the APMC as an arm of the State, and the market fee, as the tax levied by the State, rather than fee charged for providing services. This is a crucial provision which acts as a major impediment to creating national common market in agricultural commodities. Removal of this provision will pave a way for creating competition and a national common market for agricultural commodities.

Moreover, though the market fee is collected just like a tax, the revenue earned by the APMCs does not go to the state exchequer and hence does not require the approval of state legislature to utilize the funds so collected. Thus APMC operations are hidden from scrutiny.

The rate of commission charged by the licensed commission agents is exorbitant, because, unlike direct taxes which are levied on net income, the commission is charged on the entire value of the produce sold. The license fee charged from various market licensed operators is nominal, but the small number of licences granted creates a premium, which is believed to be paid in cash.

There is a perception that the positions in the market committee (at the state level) and the market board—which supervises the market committee—are occupied by the politically influential. They enjoy a cosy relationship with the licensed commission agents who wield power by exercising monopoly power within the notified area, at times by forming cartels. The resistance to reforming APMCs is perceived to be emanating from these factors.

10.4.2 Essential Commodities Act, 1955 versus APMC Act: The scope of the Essential Commodities Act (EC Act) is much broader than the APMC Act. It empowers the Central and State Governments concurrently to control production, supply and distribution of certain commodities, including pricing, stock-holding and the period for which the stocks can be kept and to impose duties. The APMC Act, on the other hand, controls only the first sale of the agricultural produce. Apart from food-stuffs which are covered under the APMC Act, the commodities covered under the EC Act generally are: drugs, fertilisers, and textiles and coal.

10.5 State Agricultural Produce Marketing (Development and Regulation) Act, 2003: The Model Act

To benefit the farming community from new market access opportunities, the internal agricultural marketing system in the country needs to be integrated and strengthened. In this context, an inter-Ministerial Task Force set up by the Ministry of Agriculture suggested a package of reform measures, such as amendments in the States' Agricultural Produce Marketing Acts to encourage development of competitive agricultural markets in the private and cooperative sectors, and deregulation of marketing system to promote private investment in marketing infrastructure.

Since the State Acts created fragment markets for

agricultural commodities and curtailed the freedom of farmers to sell their produce other than through the commission agents and other functionaries licensed by the APMCs, the Ministry of Agriculture, Government of India developed a model APMC Act, 2003 and has been pursuing the State Governments to modify their respective Acts along the lines of the Model APMC Act, 2003. The Model APMC Act: (a) provides for direct sale of farm produce to contract farming sponsors, (b) provides for setting up *special markets* for *specified agricultural commodities*—mostly perishables, (c) permits private persons, farmers and consumers to establish new markets for agricultural produce in any area, (d) requires a single levy of market fee on the sale of notified agricultural commodities in any market area, (e) replaces licensing with registration of market functionaries which would allow them to operate in one or more different market areas, (f) provides for the establishment of consumers' and farmers' markets to facilitate direct sale of agricultural produce to consumers and (g) provides for the creation of marketing infrastructure from the revenue earned by the APMC.

The model APMC Act provides some freedom to the farmers to sell their produce directly to the contract-sponsors or in the market set up by private individuals, consumers or producers. The model APMC Act also increases the competitiveness of the market of agricultural produce by allowing common registration of market intermediaries. Many of the states have partially adopted the provisions of model APMC Act and amended their APMC Acts. Some of the states have not framed rules to implement the amended provisions, which indicates hesitancy on the part of State Governments to liberalize the statutory compulsion on farmers to sell their produce through APMCs. Some states such as Karnataka have, however, adopted changes to create greater competition within state. The model law on agricultural marketing and contract farming in consultation with the State Governments and representatives of trade and industry has the following salient features:

1. Legal persons, growers and local authorities permitted to establish new markets in any area.
2. No compulsion on growers to sell their produce through existing regulated markets.
3. Establishment of direct purchase centres, consumers and farmers markets for direct sale.
4. Promotion of public-private-partnership (PPP) in the management and development of agricultural markets.
5. Separate constitution of special markets for commodities like onions, fruits, vegetables, and flowers.
6. A separate chapter to regulate and promote contract-farming arrangements in the country.
7. Prohibition of commission agency in any transaction of agricultural commodities with the producers.
8. Market Committee to promote alternative marketing system, contract farming, direct marketing and farmers and consumers markets.
9. State Marketing Boards to promote standardization, grading, quality certification, market led extension and training of farmers and market functionaries in marketing related areas.
10. Constitution of State Marketing Standards Bureau for promotion of grading, standardization and quality certification of agricultural produce.

The Government of Karnataka has taken initiative in this direction and inserted a new Chapter (Chapter XIII A) in the Karnataka Agricultural Produce Marketing (Regulation) Act 1910, to provide for the establishment of an Integrated Produce Market to be owned and managed by the National Dairy Development Board (NDDB) for marketing of fruits, vegetables and flowers in that State. Other States also need to amend respective Agricultural Produce Marketing Acts to permit any organization or corporate body to establish integrated facility for marketing of agricultural produce. Curtailment of excessive bureaucratization of markets is necessary for healthy growth of such markets.

Liberalization of world trade in agriculture has provided new opportunities to the farm sector to access markets for agricultural commodities world-wide. However, to make this happen, reforms have to be brought about in agriculture sector to remove all barriers, whether legal or policy induced, which introduce inefficiencies and monopoly rents in the functioning of agricultural markets. At present, though agricultural production is largely free from controls, the same is not true of marketing of agricultural commodities. Under the APMC Act, State Governments alone are empowered to initiate the process of setting up of markets for agriculture products within a defined area. As a result private and cooperative sectors cannot take initiative in setting up markets equipped with more modern facilities.

High investments together with entrepreneurial skills required for creation and managing the market infrastructures have to come from private sector in order to encourage private sector participation and investments required for development of alternative marketing infrastructure and supporting services, provisions of the State Agricultural Produce Marketing Regulation Act would need modification to create a lawful role for the private sector in market development. Government's role should be that of a facilitator rather than that of exercising control over the management of markets.

10.5.1 Inadequacies of Model APMC Act: The provisions of the Model APMC Act do not go far enough to create a national, or even state-level, common market for agricultural commodities. The reason is that the model APMC Act retains the mandatory requirement of the buyers having to pay APMC charges even when the produce is sold directly outside the APMC area, say, to the contract sponsors or in a market set up by private individuals even though no facility provided by the APMC is used.

Though the model APMC Act bars the APMCs and commission agents from deducting the market fee/commission from the seller, the incidence of these fees/commission falls on the farmers since buyers would discount their bids to the extent of the fees/commission charged by the APMC and the Commission agents.

Similarly, though the model APMC Act provides for setting up of markets by private sector, this provision is not adequate to create competition for APMCs even within the State, since the owner of the private market will have to collect the APMC fees/taxes, for and on behalf of the APMC, from the buyers/sellers in addition to the fee that he wants to charge for providing trading platform and other services, such as loading, unloading, grading, weighing etc.

10.6 Agricultural Marketing and Farmer Friendly Reforms Index (AMFFRI)

NITI Aayog launched in 2016 an index to rank States and UTs based on implementation of seven provisions proposed under model APMC Act like joining e-NAM initiative, special treatment to fruits and vegetables for marketing and level of taxes in mandis. These indicators reveal ease of doing agribusiness as well as opportunities for farmers to benefit from modern trade and commerce and have wider option for sale of her/his produce. These indicators also represent competitiveness, efficiency and transparency in agri markets. The second area of reforms captured by the index include facilitation and liberalization of land lease. The third area included in the index represent freedom given to farmers for felling and transit of trees grown on private land. This represent opportunity to diversify farm business.

The Index is named as Agricultural Marketing and Farmer Friendly Reforms Index (AMFFRI) and it has a score that can have minimum value 0 implying no reforms and maximum value 100 implying complete reforms in the selected areas. States and UTs have been ranked using this index.

10.6.1 Ranking of States Based on AMFFRI: No state in the country has implemented the entire set of market reforms. Also, land leasing and harvest and marketing of some tree species on private farm land are subjected to various degrees of restrictions in almost all the States/UTs. The State of Maharashtra achieved first rank in implementation of various reforms. The State has implemented most of the marketing reforms and it offers best environment for doing agri-business among all the States/UTs. Gujarat ranks second with a score of 71.5 out of 100, closely followed by Rajasthan and Madhya Pradesh.

The State of Karnataka, which is considered progressive in implementing market reforms, did not figure among the top states for two reasons. It is lagging in liberalization of land lease and restrictions on felling of trees on private land. Two, it is not yet integrated with eNAM. However, the State has its own Unified Market Platform operated by ReMS, which has all the provisions as envisaged under eNAM. If this reform in the State is treated at par with eNAM, then Karnataka earns additional score of 7.4. This increases the score of the State in AMFFRI from 55.5 to 62.9 and raises its rank from 8th place to the 6th place.

Agriculturally developed State of Punjab ranks 14th, with a score of 43.9. This is because of poor implementation of market reforms in the State.

Almost two third States/UTs could not reach even halfway mark of reforms score. Major States like U.P., Punjab, West Bengal, Assam, Jharkhand, Tamil Nadu and J&K are in this group. It is also pertinent to mention that some States/UTs do not have APMC Act. It is a challenge to provide ranking to these States in market reforms.

10.7 Forward Markets Commission (FMC)

FMC was merged with Securities and Exchange Board of India (SEBI) on September 28, 2015, to further strengthen the regulation of commodity futures market. FMC is the chief regulator of forwards and futures markets in India. It is headquartered in Mumbai and being a division of SEBI, falls within the ambit of Ministry of Finance, Government of India.

Established in 1953 under the provisions of the Forward

Contracts (Regulation) Act, 1952, it consists of 2 to 4 members, all appointed by the Government of India. Currently, the Commission allows commodity trading in 22 exchanges in India, of which 6 are national.

Just at the time the FMC was established, the Government felt that derivative markets increased speculation which led to increased costs and price instabilities. Therefore, options and futures trading was prohibited altogether in 1953.

The industry was pushed underground and the prohibition meant that development and expansion came to a halt. As futures and options markets began to develop in the rest of the world, Indian derivatives markets were left behind. The apprehensions about the role of speculation, particularly in the conditions of scarcity, prompted the Government to continue the prohibition well into the 1980s.

This left the country with a large number of small and isolated regional futures markets. The futures markets are dispersed and fragmented, with separate trading communities in different regions with little contact with one another. The exchanges generally have yet to embrace modern technology or modern business practices.

Next to the officially approved exchanges, there are many *havala* markets. Most of these unofficial commodity exchanges have operated for many decades. Some unofficial markets trade 20 to 30 times the volume of the *official* futures exchanges. They offer not only futures, but also option contracts. Transaction costs are low, and they attract many speculators and the smaller hedgers. Absence of regulation and proper clearing arrangements, however, mean that these markets are mostly *regulated* by the reputation of the main players.

The responsibilities and functions of Forward Markets Commission (FMC) are as follows:

1. To advise the Central Government in respect of the recognition or the withdrawal of recognition from any association or in respect of any other matter arising out of the administration of the Forward Contracts (Regulation)

Act, 1952.

2. To keep forward markets under observation and to take such action in relation to them, as it may consider necessary, in exercise of the powers assigned to it by or under the Act.
3. To collect and, whenever the Commission thinks it necessary, publish information regarding the trading conditions in respect of goods to which any of the provisions of the Act is made applicable, including information regarding supply, demand and prices, and to submit to the Central Government, periodical reports on the working of forward markets relating to such goods.
4. To make recommendations generally with a view to improving the organization and working of forward markets.
5. To undertake the inspection of the accounts and other documents of any recognized association or registered association or any member of such association whenever it considers it necessary.

It allows futures trading in 23 fibres and manufacturers, 15 spices, 44 edible oils, 6 pulses, 4 energy products, single vegetable, 20 metal futures, 33 others futures.

10.8 NITI Aayog on Agricultural Marketing

In the context of agricultural marketing distortions and reforms, a recent document by NITI Aayog observed, "Agricultural marketing suffers from policy distortions, fragmentation resulting from large number of intermediaries, poor infrastructure, lack of vertical integration and stranglehold of official mandis sanctioned by the Agricultural Produce Marketing Committees (APMC) acts of the states. Under the APMC acts, farmers are required to sell a large number of commodities in the vast majority of the states in a local mandi where intermediaries often manipulate the price. These same intermediaries then sell the produce to the next layer of intermediaries. Because mandis lack good storage and warehousing facilities especially when it comes to fruits and vegetables, substantial wastage occurs undermining the price received by the farmer. Mandis also charge multiple entry, exit and other fees. Therefore, it is essential that states genuinely reform their APMC acts. The Vajpayee Government had originally initiated this reform via a model APMC Act but most states have implemented it only half-heartedly. This needs to change. Several steps are required.

Reformed APMC acts should fully empower farmers to sell their produce to whomsoever they wish. In parallel, actors other than APMC mandis should be conferred the right to buy produce directly from the farmer and to set up alternative marketplaces. This will create competition and pave the way for the farmer to receive lucrative prices. Conditions also need to be created for the emergence of aggregators who would collect produce from farmers for sale in competitive marketplaces. This is necessary to serve small farmers for whom it is neither feasible nor profitable to take their produce to such markets.

While this wholesale reform may take time, following the recommendations of the committee on Encouraging Investments in Supply Chains, as an early harvest, states may exempt perishables from the APMC acts and replace licensees of APMC markets with open registration backed by bank guarantees.

There is also urgent need for restructuring the Essential Commodities Act to provide exemptions to certain categories of players such as exporters, food processors, multiple outlet retailers and large departmental retailers from applicability of stock limits. Currently, tight stock limits in many states discourage exports and development of vibrant domestic markets". [2]

To sum up, there has been limited success in establishing efficient agricultural marketing practices in India. The monopoly of government-regulated wholesale markets has prevented development of a competitive marketing system in the country. In the context of liberalization of trade in agricultural commodities and for the domestic farming community to reap the benefits of new global market access opportunities, there is a need to integrate and strengthen the internal agricultural marketing system.

Marketing of agricultural produce is the most important activity for the farming community, particularly for those who are small producers and have small surpluses for marketing. To protect the interests of farmers, Government promoted organized marketing of agricultural commodities through a network of regulated markets. However, studies indicate that the institutions of regulated markets have achieved limited success, as these markets restricted development of direct and free marketing, smooth raw material supplied to agro-processors, information exchange and adoption of innovative marketing systems and technologies.

Endnotes

1. Government of India, Ministry of Finance, *Economic Survey, 2021-22*, p. 247.
2. NITI Aayog, *India: Three Year Action Agenda (2017-18 to 2019-20)*, August 2017, p. 27-28.

11

National Agriculture Market (e-NAM)

11.1 National Market for Agricultural Commodities: What Possibility?

In his Budget (2014-15) Speech to the Parliament on July 10, 2014, the Finance Minister observed, "The farmers and consumers interest will be further served by increasing competition and integrating markets across the country. To accelerate setting up of a national market, the Central Government will work closely with the State Governments to re-orient their respective APMC Acts., to provide for establishment of private market yards/private markets. The state governments will also be encouraged to develop Farmers' Markets in town areas to enable the farmers to sell their produce directly. [1]

More steps may have to be taken and incremental moves may need to be considered to get the states on board. For example, first, it may be possible to get all the states to drop fruits and vegetables from the APMC schedule of regulated commodities; this could be followed by cereals, pulse and oil seeds, and then all remaining commodities.

State Governments should also be specifically persuaded to provide policy support for setting up infrastructure, making available land etc. for alternative or special markets in private sector, since the players in the private sector cannot viably compete with the APMCs in which the initial investment was made by the government on land and other infrastructure. In view of the difficulties in attracting domestic capital for setting up marketing infrastructure, particularly warehousing, cold storages, laboratories, grading facilities etc., liberalisation of foreign direct investment (FDI) in retail can also create the possibilities for filling in the massive investment and infrastructure deficit which results in supply-chain inefficiencies.

If persuasion fails, it may be necessary to see what the Central Government can do, taking account of the allocation of subjects under the Constitution of India. The Constitution does empower the states to enact APMC Acts under the following entries in the State List (List II) of Seventh Schedule:

Entry 14: 'Agriculture, including agricultural education and research, protection against pests and prevention of plant diseases."

Entry 26: 'Trade and Commerce within the State subject to the provisions of Entry 33 of List III' (Concurrent List).

Entry 28: 'Markets and fairs'.

However, the perception that the Constitution will have to be amended if the Centre has to play a decisive role in creating a national market remains open. There are provisions/entries in List III of the Seventh Schedule (Concurrent List) in the Constitution which can be used by the Union to enact legislation for setting up a national common market for specified agricultural commodities, viz. Entry 33 which covers trade and commerce and production, supply and distribution of foodstuffs, including edible oilseeds and oils, raw cotton, raw jute etc. Entry 42 in the Union List (List I), viz. 'Interstate Trade and Commerce' also allows a role for the Union. Once a law is passed by the Parliament to regulate trading in the specified agricultural commodities, it will override the state APMC laws, paving the way for creating a national common market. However, this approach could be seen as heavy-handed on the part of the Centre and contrary to the new spirit of co-operative federalism.

11.1.1 Unified Agriculture Marketing (UAM) Scheme: Access to markets is critical for the income of farmers. The Government is implementing the UAM Scheme which envisages a common e-market platform that will be deployed in selected 585 regulated wholesale markets. Amendments to the APMC Acts of the States are a pre-requisite to join this e-platform. 12 States have already amended their APMC Acts and are ready to come on board. More States are expected to join this platform in the coming year. The Unified Agricultural Marketing E-Platform was dedicated to the nation on the birthday of Dr. Baba Saheb Ambedkar on April 14, 2016.

11.2 National Agriculture Market (e-NAM)

Under e-NAM farmers can sell their produce on the internet.

11.2.1 What is e-NAM? e-NAM is envisaged as a pan-India electronic trading portal which seeks to network the existing APMC and other market yards to create a unified national market for agricultural commodities. e-NAM is a *virtual* market but it has a physical market (mandi) at the back end.

11.2.2 Difference between e-NAM and the Existing Mandi System: e-NAM is not a parallel marketing structure but rather a device to create a national network of physical mandis which can be accessed online. It seeks to leverage the physical infrastructure of the mandis through an online trading portal, enabling buyers situated even outside the State to participate in trading at the local level.

It was necessary to create e-NAM to facilitate the emergence of a common national market for agricultural commodities. Current APMC regulated market yards limit the scope of trading in agricultural commodities at the first point of sale (i.e. when farmers offer produce after the harvest) in the local mandi, typically at the level of *taluka/tehsil* or at best the district. Even one State is not a unified agricultural market and there are transaction costs on moving produce from one market area to another within the same State. Multiple licences are necessary to trade in different market areas in the same State. All this has led to a highly fragmented and high-cost agricultural economy, which prevents economies of scale and seamless movement of agricultural goods across district and state borders. e-NAM seeks to address and reverse this process of fragmentation of markets, ultimately lowering intermediation costs, wastage and prices for the final consumer. It builds on the strength of the local *mandi* and allows it to offer its produce at the national level.

11.2.3 Operating Mechanism of e-NAM: e-NAM electronic trading platform has been created with an investment by the Government of India (through the Ministry of Agriculture and Farmers Welfare). It offers a *plug-in* to any market yard existing in a state (whether regulated or private). The special software developed for e-NAM is available to each mandi which agrees to join the national network free of cost with necessary customization to conform to the regulations of each State Mandi Act.

States interested to integrate their mandis with e-NAM are required to carry out following reforms in their APMC Act.

1. Specific provision for electronic trading.
2. Single trading licenses valid for trading in all mandis of the State.
3. Single point levy of transaction fee.

The national level platform has been developed by the Ministry of Agriculture and Farmers Welfare, which will also bear the maintenance costs. As stated above, the integration costs for local mandis and customization of software, training etc. will also be paid for by the Ministry of Agriculture and Farmers Welfare as a one-time grant at the time of accepting the mandi in the national network. Thereafter, the running costs of the software at the local level, staff costs for quality check etc. will be met from the transaction fee to be generated through the sale of produce. The intention is to avoid any upfront investment by the mandi when it integrates into e-NAM, and also enable it to support the running cost through additional generation of revenue.

Ministry of Agriculture and Farmers Welfare, Government of India has appointed Small Farmers Agribusiness Consortium (SFAC) as the Lead Implementing Agency of e-NAM. SFAC will operate and maintain the NAM platform with the help of a strategic partner selected for the purpose.

11.2.4 Likely Benefits of e-NAM: e-NAM basically increases the choice of the farmer when he brings his produce to the mandi for sale. Local traders can bid for the produce, as also traders on the electronic platform sitting in other States. The farmer may chose to accept either the local offer or the online offer. In either case the transaction will be on the books of the local mandi and they will continue to earn the transaction fee. In fact, the volume of business will significantly increase as there will be greater competition for specific produce, resulting in higher transaction fees for the mandi.

e-NAM is envisaged as a win-win solution for all stakeholders. For the farmers, e-NAM promises more options for sale at his nearest mandi. For the local trader in the mandi, e-NAM offers the opportunity to access a larger national market for secondary trading. Bulk buyers, processors, exporters etc. benefit from being able to participate directly in trading at the local mandi level through the e-NAM platform, thereby reducing their intermediation costs. The gradual integration of all the major mandis in the States into e-NAM will ensure common procedures for issue of licenses, levy of fee and movement of produce. In the near future we can expect significant benefits through higher returns to farmers, lower transaction costs to buyers and stable prices and availability to consumers. The e-NAM will also facilitate the emergence of integrated value chains in major agricultural commodities across the country and help to promote scientific storage and movement of agri commodities.

So far, Ministry of Agriculture and Farmers Welfare, GoI, has accorded in principle approval to the proposals of 12 States /UTs for integration of 365 mandis with e-NAM. More and more states are expected to integrate with e-NAM. There is a large number of agricultural commodities being traded on e-NAM.

As regards the functioning of e-NAM, a NITI Aayog document commented, "Agricultural market in India is highly fragmented. With each farmer confined to a single mandi in many products in many states, we currently have thousands of markets across which no arbitrage takes place. This represents a huge inefficiency in the system, which must be corrected. Launched in April 2016, electronic-National Agricultural Market (e-NAM) is an important initiative in this direction. The initiative aims to unify mandis across the nation into a single national market through electronic trading whereby a buyer located anywhere in India would be able to place an order in any mandi in India. Though it currently covers more than 400 markets and is to be extended to 585 mandis by the end of 2017-18 and progress has been made in smoothing out transactions within participating mandis, cross-mandi purchases are few and far between. Even in Karnataka, which has pioneered the idea, with rare exceptions, sales within a mandi are confined to buyers who are physically present. Buyers show a strong preference for physical inspection of grain over quality assessment through assaying while farmers are reported to fear that assaying reduces the price of their produce. More work is required. Necessary measures include third party assaying and quality certification mechanisms, dispute settlement mechanisms, systems for forwarding goods to buyers, digital infrastructure to enable the national market and encouragement of FPOs. These are all key building blocks of a successful e-NAM, and we must ensure that they come into being alongside the platform". [2]

11.2.5 e-NAM in the 2018-19 Budget: In connection with e-NAM, late Finance Minister Arun Jaitley in his budget speech to the Parliament on February 1, 2018 observed, "...last year, I had announced strengthening of e-NAM and to expand coverage of e-NAM to 585 APMCs. 470 APMCs have been connected to e-NAM network and rest will be connected by March, 2018.

More than 86 percent of our farmers are small and marginal. They are not always in a position to directly transact at APMCs and other wholesale markets. We will develop and upgrade existing 22,000 rural *haats* into Gramin Agricultural Markets (GrAMs). In these GrAMs, physical infrastructure will be strengthened using MGNREGA and other Government schemes. These GrAMs, electronically linked to e-NAM and exempted from regulations of APMCs, will provide farmers facility to make direct sale to consumers and bulk purchasers.

An Agri-Market Infrastructure Fund with a corpus of ₹ 2,000 crore will be set up for developing and upgrading agricultural marketing infrastructure in the 22,000 Grameen Agricultural Markets (GrAMs) and 585 APMCs.

Task of connecting all eligible habitations with an all-weather road has been substantially completed, with the target date brought forward to March 2019 from March 2022. It is now time to strengthen and widen its ambit further to include major link routes which connect habitations to agricultural and rural markets (GrAMs), higher secondary schools and hospitals. Prime Minister Gram Sadak Yojana Phase III will include such linkages". [3]

To conclude, Government of India launched National Agriculture Market (e-NAM) Scheme in 2016 with the objective of creating online transparent competitive bidding system to facilitate farmers with remunerative prices for their produce. Under the e-NAM Scheme, government is providing free software and assistance of ₹ 75 lakh per APMC mandi for related hardware including quality assaying equipment and creation of infrastructure like cleaning, grading, sorting, packaging and compost unit etc.

Further, a Central Sector Scheme of "Formation and Promotion of 10,000 Farmer Producer Organizations (FPOs)" was launched to form and promote 10,000 new FPOs till 2027-28. Under the scheme, the formation and promotion of FPO is based on Produce Cluster Area approach and specialized commodity-based approach. While adopting cluster-based approach, formation of FPOs focuses on *One District One Product* to enable product specialization. One of the objectives of the scheme is to enhance productivity through efficient, cost-effective and sustainable resource use and realize higher returns through better liquidity and market linkages for their produce and to become sustainable through collective action.

As of January 2022, a total of 1963 FPOs have been registered under the scheme. Government established a full-fledged Ministry of Co-operation in July 2021 with a view to provide greater focus to the cooperative sector.

Endnotes

1. Government of India, Ministry of Finance, Budget Papers 2014-15, Speech of the Finance Minister, July 10, 2014, para 82.
2. NITI Aayog, *India: Three Year Action Agenda (2017-18 to 2019-20)*, August 2017, p. 28.
3. Government of India, Ministry of Finance, Budget Papers (2018-19), *Speech of the Finance Minister*, paras 16 to 18.

12

Minimum Support Prices (MSP) and Food Stocks

The main policy measures in the agriculture sector were adopted in the mid-1960s. These included minimum support prices, subsidies, public storage, procurement and distribution of foodgrains, and trade protection measures. During the 1960s and 1970s, widespread adoption of high yielding rice and wheat varieties occurred. The country also expanded irrigated areas, promoted increased use of chemical fertilizers and pesticides, and improved access to institutional credit. Together, all these initiatives led to considerable rise in agricultural production making India self-sufficient in foodgrains production at the national level.

12.1 Objectives of Agricultural Price Policy

For the large sections of the community which live near the margin of subsistence, a certain minimum supply of foodgrains at reasonable prices constitutes the rock-bottom of the standard of living, a fall in which would be seriously detrimental to health and efficiency. Foodgrains occupy a pivotal place in the price structure, and if this latter has to be safeguarded, the prices of foodgrains must be held stable at levels within the reach of the poorer sections of the community.

The objectives of a sound agricultural price policy are two-fold: (a) to ensure fair prices for the produce of the farmers and (b) to ensure adequate and regular supply of agricultural commodities to the consumers at reasonable prices. Excessive fluctuations in agricultural prices generate harmful effects both for the producers and the consumers. The beneficiaries of unstable prices are the middlemen and the speculators. It is for these reasons that Government undertakes buffer stocks operations, i.e. making purchases when there is glut of produce in the market and releasing stocks during period of scarcity. The price policy also seeks to evolve a balanced and integrated price structure in the perspective of the overall needs of the economy.

Towards this end, the government announces each season the minimum support prices (MSP) for major agricultural commodities and organizes purchase operations through public, cooperative and other agencies designated by the state governments. The co-operative societies and government agencies have helped the farmers to escape the exploitative practices of the private traders.

12.2 Minimum Support Prices (MSP)

An important element of the agricultural price policy of the Government of India is the announcement every year of MSP for major commodities.

Assurance of a remunerative and stable price environment is considered very important for increasing agricultural production and productivity since the market place for agricultural produce tends to be inherently unstable, which often inflicts undue losses on the growers, even when they adopt the best available technology package and produce efficiently. Towards this end, MSP for major agricultural products are fixed by the Government, each year, after taking into account the recommendations of CACP. [1]

12.2.1 Historical Perspective: As a result of the partition of India in 1947, the balance between foodgrains availability and population was disturbed, leading to food shortages in new India. Therefore, the First Five Year Plan (1951-52 to 1955-56) was mainly devoted to agricultural development. The recurring scarcities and shortages of essential food items forced the Government to adopt an elaborate system of public procurement and distribution of foodgrains. For this purpose, the Food Corporation of India (FCI) was established in 1965, and a price support system for major agricultural crops was introduced. In spite of certain drawbacks, the system worked reasonably well till the late 1970s. Since then, production of foodgrains in the country has kept pace with the requirements of the population, owing mainly to the spread of new technology among farmers.

The price support policy of the Government is directed at providing insurance to agricultural producers against any sharp fall in farm prices. MSP are virtually minimum guaranteed prices fixed by the Government for various crops.

Till the mid-1970s, Government announced two types of administered prices: (a) minimum support prices (MSP) and (b) procurement prices.

MSP served as the floor prices and were fixed by the Government in the nature of a long-term guarantee for investment decisions of producers, with the assurance that prices of their commodities would not be allowed to fall below the level fixed by the government, even in the case of a bumper crop.

Procurement prices were the prices of kharif and rabi cereals at which these were domestically procured by public agencies like the Food Corporation of India (FCI) for release through public distribution system (PDS). They were announced soon after the harvest began. Normally, procurement prices were lower than the open market prices and higher than the MSP.

This policy of two official prices continued, with some variations, up to 1973-74, in the case of paddy. In the case of wheat, it was discontinued in 1969 and then revived in 1974-75 for 1 year only. Since there were too many demands for stepping up the MSP, the present system was evolved in 1975 in which only one set of prices is announced for paddy (and other kharif crops) and wheat (and other rabi crops).

12.2.2 Methodology for Cost Calculation: The minimum support prices for major agricultural products are announced each year after taking into account the recommendations of the CACP. The Union Budget for 2018-19 had announced the pre-determined principle to keep MSP at the level of one and half times of the cost of production. Accordingly, government had increased the MSP for all mandated kharif, rabi and other commercial crops with a return of at least 50 per cent over all India weighted average cost of production from the agricultural year 2018-19 onwards.

While recommending price policy of various commodities, CACP takes into account all important factors including the following:

1. Cost of production.
2. Changes in input prices.
3. Input/output price parity.
4. Trends in market prices, both domestic and international.
5. Inter-crop price parity.
6. Demand and supply situation.
7. Terms of trade between agricultural and non-agricultural sectors. [2]
8. Likely implications of MSP on consumers of that product.

Among these multiple factors that go into the formulation of support price policy, the cost of production is the most significant. Thus, for making the support price policy functionally meaningful, the minimum guaranteed prices ought to cover cost of production plus return on investments.

CACP analyses cost of production data for various states in respect of various commodities. With costs of production for the same crops varying between regions and also across farms within the same region and for different producers, the level of costs that could be accepted as a norm poses enormous difficulties.

Broadly speaking, there are two concepts of cost of production, namely A2 + FL and C2.

A2 + FL measure takes into account the following cost components:

1. Value of agricultural inputs such as seeds, fertilizers, insecticides etc.
2. Hired human, animal and machine labour.
3. Land revenue.
4. Irrigation charges.
5. Depreciation of farm implements and buildings.
6. Interest on working capital.

7. Rent paid for leased in land.
8. Imputed value of family labour.

C2 measure, in addition to A2 + FL, also includes imputed value of rent on land owned by the cultivator.

Based on the recommendations of M.S. Swaminathan Committee, farmers had demanded MSP at 1.5 times the comprehensive measure of cultivation costs (C2). The government uses a narrow measure (A2 + FL).

In fact, MSP policy has three integrated components:

1. MSP based on cost + 50 percent formula.
2. All farmers receive the MSP as promised.
3. Safe storage and efficient distribution network.

Experience has it that government procurement based on MSP is limited to paddy in the kharif (summer) season and wheat in the rabi (winter) season. It has a demanding task for procurement, safe storage and distribution.

12.2.3 Crops Covered under MSP: Presently, CACP recommends MSP of the following 23 commodities:

1. 7 cereals (paddy, wheat, maize, sorghum, pearl millet, barley and ragi).
2. 5 pulses (gram, tur, moong, urad, lentil).
3. 7 oilseeds (groundnut, rapeseed-mustard, soyabean, seasmum, sunflower, safflower, nigerseed).
4. 4 commercial crops (copra, sugarcane, cotton and raw jute).

The decision on MSP is taken by the Cabinet Committee on Economic Affairs chaired by the Prime Minister.

MSP are federally fixed prices for form produce aimed at preventing distress sale. The government buys agriculture produce (mainly rice and wheat) largely at these prices through its procurement agencies. The varying hikes in MSP for different crops are aimed at correcting crop imbalances and promoting crop diversification.

As regards MSP, Finance Minister Arun Jaitley in his budget speech to the Parliament on February 1, 2018 announced, "...in our party's manifesto it has been stated that the farmers should realize at least 50 percent more than the cost of their produce, in other words, one and a half times of the cost of their production. Government has been very much sensitive to this resolutions and it has declared minimum support price (MSP) for the majority of rabi crops at least at one and a half times the cost involved. Now, we have decided to implement this resolution as a principle for the rest of crops. I am pleased to announce that as per pre-determined principle, the government has decided to keep MSP for the all unannounced crops of kharif at least at one and half times of their production cost. I am confident that this historic decision will prove an important step towards doubling the income of our farmers". [3]

12.2.4 Minimum Support Prices (MSP) for Kharif Crops: As follow up action to provide farmers a profit margin of at least 50 percent over their cost of production for all the notified crops across the country, the government announces MSP for 14 kharif (or summer or monsoon) crops usually in the first week of June. Kharif crops harvest starts in October.

On June 8, 2022, the Cabinet Committee on Economic Affairs (CCEA) approved the increase in MSP for all mandated kharif crops for marketing season 2022-23. Table 12.1 presents MSP for select kharif crops for 2022-23 marketing season.

Table 12.1: Minimum Support Prices (MSP) for Select Kharif Crops for 2022-23 Marketing Season

(₹ per quintal)

Crop	2021-22	2022-23
Paddy (common variety)	1,940	2,040
Maize	1,870	1,962
Groundnut	5,550	5,550
Cotton (medium staple)	5,726	6,080

Source: Government of India, Ministry of Agriculture and Farmers Welfare.

Millets (jowar, bajra, ragi) are less-water-consuming and climate resilient. Due to their high nutritional value, the government has notified them as *nutri-cereals*. Conversely, paddy is a water-guzzling crop.

The message of the new MSP regime was to encourage farmers to cultivate pulses, millets and oilseeds. Pulses and millets will ensure nutritional security while more oilseeds production will help reduce the import bill.

12.2.5 Minimum Support Prices (MSP) for Rabi Crops: On September 8, 2021, the government announced MSP for all mandated of rabi (or winter-sown) crops, the procurement of which will begin sometime around April 2022.

The policy of the government is to ensure minimum 50 percent return to farmers over cost of production of all notified crops. MSP were announced for wheat, gram, lentils, rapeseeds, mustard and safflower. The increase in MSP was in line with the recommendations of the Swaminathan Commission.

Table 12.2 shows the MSP of various rabi crops for the years 2021-22 and 2022-23.

Table 12.2: Minimum Support Prices (MSP) for Various Rabi Crops for 2022-23 Marketing Season

(₹ per quintal)

Crop	2021-22	2022-23
Wheat	1,975	2,015
Barley	1,600	1,635
Gram	5,100	5,230
Masur (lentils)	5,100	5,500
Rapeseed and mustard	4,650	5,050
Safflower	5,327	5,441

Source: Government of India, Ministry of Agriculture and Farmers Welfare.

12.3 Economic Cost of Foodgrains to Food Corporation of India (FCI)

The economic cost of foodgrains to FCI is of strategic importance, as it influences not only the food subsidy bill but also the country's competitiveness in international markets for foodgrains. The FCI is reimbursed the difference between the economic cost of foodgrains and the issue price. The economic cost of foodgrains to FCI has been on the rise over the years. The increase in the MSP of rice and wheat, and the rising trend in distribution costs have contributed to the increase in the economic costs of foodgrains over the years.

MSP lay the floor for the market price of foodgrains, especially the two dominant foodgrains: rice and wheat. With sharp increases in MSP every year despite surpluses having replaced shortages, the MSP have become the maximum selling price instead of being the floor price. This coupled with the system of open-ended procurement has made FCI the buyer of the first resort resulting in huge accumulation of surplus public stocks of foodgrains, leading to much higher commitments for Government subsidy. FCI has thus become the main buyer, stockist and seller in the domestic market. It is also the main exporter.

High statutory levies (including mandi charges, cesses and fees to commission agents) on grain purchase, not only discourage private trade but also increase FCI's cost, thus putting a pressure on the food subsidy bill. The levies imposed by the State Governments (ad valorem) differ from State to State and are highest in case of Punjab, Haryana and Andhra Pradesh.

The High Level Committee on Long Term Grain Policy recommended that Government may, for open-ended procurement, in future announce a gross price, inclusive of MSP and a uniform 4 percent allowance for State taxes as the price that its agencies would be allowed to pay. It would be better for the centre and states to agree on a ceiling on statutory levies, and announce MSP which farmers could actually expect to receive net of all compulsory levies.

12.4 Assessment of Minimum Support Prices (MSP)

MSP lay the floor for the market price of foodgrains, especially the two dominant foodgrains: rice and wheat. With sharp increases in MSP every year despite surpluses having replaced shortages, the MSP has become the maximum selling price instead of being the floor price. This coupled with the system of open-ended procurement has made FCI the buyer of the first resort resulting in huge accumulation of surplus public stocks of foodgrains, leading to much higher commitments for government subsidy. FCI has thus become the main buyer, stockiest and seller in the domestic market. It is also the main exporter.

12.4.1 Negative Fallouts of MSP Policy: In recent years, with the MSP announced by the Government at levels higher than those recommended by the CACP, procurement has been high and off-take low, resulting in an inevitable build-up of stocks and a bloated food subsidy bill. The macro implications of burgeoning food stocks are manifold but the following two are more important. Firstly, higher procurement, along with additional storage and maintenance costs, means higher food subsidy which increases deficit on the already strained revenue account of the Central Government. Secondly, since food stocks are financed by preferential food credit, they have monetary implications as well. Higher demand for food credit can give rise to possible crowding-out effects on other sectors. In view of the present high level of food security, there is need to focus on the distributional aspects of foodgrains rather than encouraging unsustainable levels of cereal production and procurement through the MSP.

The other negative fallouts of the declared MSP may be summarised as follows:

1. Since the issue price and the purchase price are linked, higher purchase prices result in higher issue prices. Further, with a large part of the marketed surplus in FCI warehouses, the lower supply exerts an upward pressure on prices in the open market. Everyone, except those farmers with marketable surpluses of foodgrains, is affected adversely.
2. High MSP combined with open-ended purchases by FCI has almost eliminated private wholesale trade and storage

with lower incidental and storage costs in foodgrains.

3. Exclusive attention to wheat and rice has distorted the cropping pattern of farmers in favour of these two foodgrains alone.
4. Higher water and fertilizer intensity of these two crops has had adverse environmental impacts.
5. Concentration of FCI purchases in just two foodgrains and in few States has facilitated tax exportation by some of these States. Although necessities like foodgrains are normally kept outside the tax net, Punjab and Haryana have imposed taxes such as mandi fees on the purchases of foodgrains. With FCI paying such taxes, the tax gets exported to consumers in other States.
6. High statutory levies (including mandi charges, cesses and fees to commission agents) on grain purchase, not only discourage private trade but also increase FCI's cost, thus putting a pressure on the food subsidy bill. The levies imposed by the State Governments (ad valorem) differ from State to State and are highest in case of Punjab, Haryana and Andhra Pradesh. The High Level Committee on Long Term Grain Policy recommended that government may, for open-ended procurement, in future announce a gross price, inclusive of MSP and a uniform 4 percent allowance for State taxes as the price that its agencies would be allowed to pay. It would be better for the centre and states to agree on a ceiling on statutory levies, and announce MSP which farmers could actually expect to receive net of all compulsory levies.
7. Shortage of storage space has pushed up costs through wastage and deterioration of stocks.
8. High carrying cost is a subsidy benefiting neither the consumers nor the producers.
9. There are severe regional imbalances in the operation of the entire food subsidy scheme, as FCI's purchase operations are mainly confined to five areas, viz. Punjab, Haryana, Western Uttar Pradesh, Andhra Pradesh and

Chhattisgarh. The implication for the present policy of purchase is that farmers of only a few States get the entire farmers' subsidy. A large percentage of these farmers are not even poor.

12.4.2 Realistic MSP: It is of paramount importance to set more realistic MSP, particularly with respect to wheat. To conform to its true nature, the MSP should correspond to the CACP-determined C2 cost, which includes all cash costs and imputed cost of family labour. Since these estimates may vary across regions, a simple average of these costs should be used as the uniform MSP.

12.4.3 Open-ended versus Close-ended Purchase Operations: The purchase operations should not be open-ended. Before every sowing season, procurement targets should be fixed on the basis of norms and a margin of error of about 10 percent. FCI should suspend purchase operations once targets are achieved. The FCI should have the flexibility of adding to these target quantities in specific markets only in case overall procurements fall short of the target in other markets. A system of price insurance, similar to the Farm Income Insurance Programme introduced recently on a pilot basis, may be developed. The scheme should be self-financing and without any subsidy obligation. This can operate in conjunction with the purchase operations to benefit those farmers who miss out on the opportunity of selling their surplus at the support price because of the close-ended purchase operations.

12.4.4 Decentralised Procurement Operations: The decentralised procurement scheme of the Government of India is in operation since 1997. Under this scheme, the designated States procure, store and also issue foodgrains as per allotments indicated by the Central Government under TPDS. The difference between the economic cost of the State Governments and the Central Issue Price is passed on to the State Governments as subsidy. The decentralised system of procurement, apart from helping to cover more farmers under the MSP of the Central Government, has the merit of economising the transport and administrative costs involved in procurement and distribution operations. Further, it helps in minimising the dependence of State Governments on the FCI for PDS requirements and reducing the complaints about quality, as consuming States themselves are the custodians of the procured foodgrains. However, the scheme has evoked limited response from the State Governments.

The concerns of the State Governments broadly relate to financing of operations (RBI valuation norms for stocks of foodgrains) and reimbursement of expenses and release of subsidy by the Central Government (fixation of economic cost of foodgrains of State Governments and delays in the release of the subsidy). The concerns relating to the reimbursement of expenses and release of subsidy have been largely addressed through a process of consultation of the stakeholders concerned. On the request of the States, the issues relating to valuation norms have been taken up with the RBI.

To quote, "In the short-run, decentralization of procurement may not be a practical option. However, it should be pursued as a long-run objective to usher in greater efficiency in the purchase and distribution operations, and to distribute the benefits of the price support operations more evenly across the country. A useful approach can be to work out the details of the scheme and announce it as soon as possible, allowing States to join in at the time of their choice. Once the farmers of non-participating States appreciate the benefits of their States joining in, the political process should ensure participation of a growing number of States. Eventually, the FCI should act only as a coordinating agency in the matter of procurement with important parameters like procurement prices and aggregate stock requirements provided by the Government of India. In the meantime, the FCI should include a greater number of States in their price-support operations. Further, the tendency for tax exportation needs to be curbed, by appropriate legislation, if necessary. Since it is easy to identify the States that indulge in this practice, it should also be possible to work out differential purchase prices for individual States based on the basic price and maximum allowed tax on the price". [4]

12.4.5 Normative versus Actual Unit Costs: In order to enforce efficiency, the reimbursement of costs to FCI should be based on normative unit costs and actual quantity involved, instead of reimbursement on actual basis. If some of the functions of the FCI can be carried out by others, it would help to trim the unwieldy size of the FCI. For example, actual delivery of grain may be postponed at the time of purchase, and a small mark-up on the purchase price may be allowed for this purpose. This will reduce the burden of storage on FCI. Active participation by private traders can also relieve the burden on FCI, but necessary institutional changes, including a revision of the concerned laws, are pre-requisites. The responsibility for losses will have to be put squarely on the personnel above a given level, with general cuts in staff payments and perquisites. To balance this, costs reduced below norm-based ones may be retained and distributed among the staff as annual bonus or any other mechanism deemed fit.

As regards MSP, a NITI Aayog document observed, "MSP has distorted cropping patterns, with excessive focus on the cultivation of wheat, rice and sugarcane in the procurement states at the expense of other crops such as pulses, oilseed and coarse grains. It has also resulted in depletion of water resources, soil degradation and deterioration in water quality in some states, especially in the north-western region. At the same time it has discriminated against eastern states where procurement at the MSP is minimal or non-existent. One measure that can help remove distortion in the MSP system to some degree is the system of "Price Deficiency Payment". While MSP may still be used for need-based procurement, under the deficiency payments system, a subsidy would be provided on other targeted produce in case the price falls below an MSP-linked threshold. This approach would not require procurement and thereby preventing the accumulation of unwanted stocks. More importantly, it would spread price incentives to producers in all the regions and all the crops considered important for providing price support. Each farmer would register her crop and acreage sown with the nearest APMC mandi. If the market price then falls below the floor price, the farmer would be entitled to the difference up to a maximum of, say, 10 percent of the MSP-linked price that could be paid via Direct Benefit Transfer (DBT) into an Aadhaar-linked bank account. This system would keep the quantum of the subsidy in some check and also meet the restrictions on the subsidy imposed by the World Trade Organization (WTO). The system can initially be piloted in one or two crops in a few districts". [5]

In short, when planting crops, farmers face several uncertainties in terms of the future prices of their produce. In principle, a farmer could buy an option contract to reduce this price uncertainty and make corresponding cropping decisions, but in reality this option is unavailable for all but a miniscule fraction of India's farmers. Instead, future prices are guaranteed by the government through the MSP. Although Government announces MSP for 23 crops, effective MSP-linked procurement occurs mainly for wheat, rice and cotton. While there is no Government procurement per se in sugarcane, a crop with assured irrigation, mills are legally obligated to buy cane from farmers at prices fixed by Government, an effective MSP-like engagement.

Government's price policy for agricultural produce seeks to ensure remunerative prices to growers for their produce with a view to encouraging higher investment and production and safeguarding the interests of consumers by making available food supplies at reasonable prices. The price policy also seeks to evolve a balanced and integrated price structure in keeping with the overall needs of the economy. To achieve this end, the government announces minimum support prices (MSP) for major agricultural commodities each season and organizes purchase operations through the Food Corporation of India, and cooperative and other agencies designated by state governments. The government decides on the MSP for various agricultural commodities taking into account the recommendations of the Commission for Agricultural Costs and Prices (CACP), the views of State Governments and Central Ministries as well as such other relevant factors which are considered important for fixation of support prices.

The estimates of cost of cultivation and cost of production of important agricultural crops covered under the mechanism of MSP are made by the Commission for Agricultural Costs and Prices (CACP) which recommends the MSP to the Government. Price policy for agricultural commodities reflects an important element of overall agricultural policy.

Government decides on the support price for various agricultural commodities taking into account the recommendations of the CACP, the views of State Governments and Central Ministries as well as such other relevant factors which, in the opinion of the Government, are important for fixation of support prices.

While in principle MSP exists for most farmers for most crops, its realistic impact is quite limited for most farmers in the country. Public procurement at MSP has disproportionately focused on wheat, rice and sugarcane and perhaps even at the expense of other crops such as pulses and oilseeds. This has resulted in buffer stocks of paddy and wheat to be above the required norms, but also caused frequent price spikes in pulses and edible oils, despite substantial imports of these commodities.

The absence of MSP procurement for most crops in most states implies either that farmers are selling their products to private intermediaries above the MSP or the converse, i.e. farmers have little option but to sell their produce at prices below the MSP, resulting in a regional bias in farm incomes. There is a general sense that the latter is a more prevalent phenomenon, highlighting the need for reorienting agriculture price policies, such that MSP are matched by public procurement efforts towards crops that better reflect the country's natural resource scarcities.

12.5 Burgeoning Food Stocks

As a result of the partition of India in 1947, the balance between foodgrains availability and population was disturbed, leading to food shortages in new India. Therefore, the First Five Year Plan (1951-56) was mainly devoted to agricultural development. The recurring scarcities and shortages of essential food items forced the Government to adopt an elaborate system of public procurement and distribution of foodgrains.

For this purpose, the Food Corporation of India (FCI) was established in 1965, and a price support system for major agricultural crops was introduced. In spite of certain drawbacks, the system worked reasonably well till the late 1970s. Since then, production of foodgrains in the country has kept pace with the requirements of the population, owing mainly to the spread of new technology among farmers.

Government takes special measures, such as release of foodgrains from the FCI at concessional rates for exports, offloading of the old and low quality foodgrains through tender sale and reduction in the APL issue price to bring back APL population to the PDS fold, to dispose of the excess stock of foodgrains. These measures help in reducing the excess stock of foodgrains with the FCI.

12.5.1 Buffer Stock Operations: Excessive fluctuations in agricultural prices generate harmful effects both for the producers and the consumers. The beneficiaries of unstable prices are the middlemen and the speculators. It is for these reasons that Government undertakes buffer stocks operations, i.e. making purchases when there is glut of produce in the market and releasing stocks during period of scarcity.

Periodically, an official committee is set up to recommend the volume of minimum buffer stocks to be maintained at the beginning of each quarter for the purpose of food security.

This quantum, together with the amount needed to run the PDS, constitutes the minimum operational stocks of the FCI. However, the purchases of the FCI are open-ended in that it has to accept all the grains that are sold to it at the declared purchase price, and this sometimes results in mounting stocks well beyond the buffer stock norms.

The rising MSP for rice and wheat induce the farmers to cultivate these two crops more than other crops. Increased production of rice and wheat leads to their higher procurement by official agencies which, in turn, results in large accumulation of Government food stocks. On the other hand, the off-take of foodgrains through PDS is relatively low due to the following reasons.

1. Narrow price differential between the open market price and the price at which foodgrains are made available through the PDS.
2. Altered consumption pattern of the population (towards milk, eggs and meat as against cereals) owing to improved income levels.
3. Lacklustre export performance of agricultural products.

The off-take from the PDS appears to be poor especially in some States like Bihar. It could be due to the fact that the economic cost has been going up, the prices at which foodgrains are supplied to people below the poverty line are also going up, and have become unaffordable to the poor in the category. It could also be due to the poor quality of the foodgrains supplied through the PDS. Besides, the quantities supplied at subsidised prices are not adequate for the sustenance of the whole family, and people have to supplement them by purchase from the open market. Thus, the implementation of the PDS does not seem to be serving the purpose of making foodgrains available to people at affordable prices.

Large stocks of foodgrains raise the subsidy bill through increased handling and carrying costs along with the losses. Besides, withdrawing such large quantities from the market also results in rising open market prices of foodgrains, neutralising much of the consumer benefits that the subsidy provides.

MSP lay the floor for the market price of foodgrains, especially the two dominant foodgrains: rice and wheat. With sharp increases in MSP every year despite surpluses having replaced shortages, the MSP have become the maximum selling price instead of being the floor price. This coupled with the system of open-ended procurement has made FCI the buyer of the first resort resulting in huge accumulation of surplus public stocks of foodgrains, leading to much higher commitments for Government subsidy. FCI has thus become the main buyer, stockist and seller in the domestic market. It is also the main exporter.

12.5.2 Macro Implications: The macro implications of burgeoning food stocks are manifold but the following two are more important. Firstly, higher procurement, along with additional storage and maintenance costs, means higher food subsidy which increases deficit on the already strained revenue account of the Central Government. Secondly, since food stocks are financed by preferential food credit, they have monetary implications as well. Higher demand for food credit can give rise to possible crowding-out effects on other sectors.

In view of the present high level of food security, there is need to focus on the distributional aspects of foodgrains rather than encouraging unsustainable levels of cereal production and procurement through the MSP.

12.5.3 Decentralised Procurement Scheme: The decentralised procurement scheme of the Government of India is in operation since 1997. Under this scheme, the designated States procure, store and also issue foodgrains as per allotments indicated by the Central Government under Targeted Public Distribution System (TPDS). The difference between the economic cost of the State Governments and the Central Issue Price is passed on to the State Governments as subsidy. The decentralised system of procurement, apart from helping to cover more farmers under the MSP of the Central Government, has the merit of economising the transport and administrative costs involved in procurement and distribution operations. Further, it helps in minimising the dependence of State Governments on the FCI for PDS requirements and reducing the complaints about quality, as consuming States themselves are the custodians of the procured foodgrains.

However, the scheme has evoked limited response from the State Governments. At present, the State Governments of West Bengal, Madhya Pradesh, Uttar Pradesh, Chhattisgarh, Uttarakhand and Tamil Nadu are implementing this scheme in a limited way. The States of Assam and Nagaland and the Union Territory of Andaman and Nicobar Islands have also evinced interest in the scheme.

The concerns of the State Governments broadly relate to financing of operations and reimbursement of expenses and delays in the release of subsidy by the Central Government.

12.6 Storage of Foodgrains

India runs one of the largest food management programmes in the world. India's food management programme includes food procurement, allocation, storage and the issue of food subsidy along with various government measures for effective food and nutritional security.

The major objectives of food management are procurement of foodgrains from farmers at remunerative prices, distribution of foodgrains to consumers, particularly the vulnerable sections of society at affordable prices and maintenance of food buffer stock for food security and price stability. The instruments used are procurement at MSP from farmers and sale at Central Issue Price (CIP) under the Targeted Public Distribution System (TPDS). The nodal agency which undertakes procurement, distribution and storage of foodgrains is the Food Corporation of India (FCI). The distribution of foodgrains is undertaken primarily under the National Food Security Act, 2013 (NFSA) and other welfare schemes of the Government of India.

The storage capacity available with FCI, a part of warehousing capacity available with Central Warehousing Corporation (CWC) and State Warehousing Corporations (SWCs) and capacity hired from private sector is used for storage of foodgrains procured for central pool by the government agencies.

Government is implementing a Central Sector Scheme for construction of godowns with focus on augmenting storage capacity in the States of North Eastern (NE) Region and a few other States. Under this Scheme, funds are released directly to FCI in the form of equity for land acquisition and construction of storage godowns and infrastructure like railway sidings, electrification, installation of weighbridge etc. Funds are also released as grants-in-aid to the governments of the North-Eastern States including Jammu & Kashmir for construction of intermediate storage godowns considering the storage gaps as well as difficult geographical and climatic conditions in these States.

Government of India has also approved an action plan/road map for construction of steel silos in the country in Public Private Partnership (PPP) mode for modernizing storage infrastructure and improving shelf life of stored foodgrains.

Endnotes

1. Agricultural Prices Commission came into existence in January 1965. It was renamed as Commission for Agricultural Costs and Prices (CACP) in 1985. CACP is an attached office of the Ministry of Agriculture and Farmers Welfare, Government of India. It is mandated to recommend minimum support prices (MSP) to incentivize the cultivators to adopt modern technology, and raise productivity and overall grain production in linc with the emerging demand patterns in the country.

   CACP submits its recommendations to the Government in the form of Price Policy Reports every year, separately for five groups of commodities, namely Kharif crops, Rabi crops, sugarcane, raw jute and copra.

   Before preparing aforesaid five pricing policy reports, CACP draws a comprehensive questionnaire, and sends it to all the

State Governments and concerned national organizations and Ministries to seek their views. Subsequently, separate meetings are also held with farmers from different states, state governments, national organizations like FCI, NAFED, Cotton Corporation of India (CCI), Jute Corporation of India (JCI), traders' organizations, processing organizations, and key Central Ministries. CACP also makes visits to states for on-the-spot assessment of the various constraints that farmers face in marketing their produce, or even raising the productivity levels of their crops. Based on all these inputs, CACP finalizes its recommendations/reports, which are then submitted to the Government. The Government, in turn, circulates the CACP reports to State Governments and concerned Central Ministries for their comments. After receiving the feed-back from them, the Cabinet Committee on Economic Affairs (CCEA) of the Union Government takes a final decision on the level of MSP and other recommendations made by CACP. Once this decision is taken, CACP puts all its reports on the web site for various stakeholders to see the rationale behind price and non-price recommendations of the CACP.

2. Terms of trade between the agricultural and non-agricultural sectors is a subject of controversy among agricultural economists in India. Terms of trade are defined as the ratio of agricultural prices to non-agricultural prices. There are two schools of thought. According to one, terms of trade have moved in favour of the agricultural sector with the result that the development of the industrial sector has slowed down. Hence, it is contended that agricultural prices should be lowered to give a boost to industries.

   Contrarily, many hold the view that terms of trade have moved against the farm sector and therefore higher agricultural prices are needed to induce the farmers to produce more. The debate is inconclusive because the results of various studies are conflicting due to different methodologies and assumptions adopted by the researchers.

   Realising the importance of inter-sectoral terms of trade, the Government of India modified the terms of reference for CACP. Consequently, CACP has been regularly taking into account the terms of trade ever since 1980 while recommending support/procurement prices for agricultural commodities.

In the meantime, Government of India constituted a Task Force in March 1993 (Chairman: A.S. Kahlon) to suggest methodology for constructing an index of terms of trade between agricultural and non-agricultural sectors. The Government now computes the terms of trade between the two sectors on the basis of the methodology recommended by the Task Force. For more details on the index of terms of trade between the agricultural and non-agricultural sectors, see Reserve Bank of India, *Report on Currency and Finance*, 1998-99, pp. III-4 and 5.

3. Government of India, Ministry of Finance, Budget Papers (2018-19), *Speech of the Finance Minister*, paras 13 to 15.
4. Government of India, Ministry of Finance, *Central Government Subsidies in India*, December 2004, p. 13.
5. NITI Aayog, *India: Three Year Action Agenda (2017-18 to 2019-20)*, August 2017, pp. 28-29.

13

Food Subsidy and Public Distribution System (PDS)

Foodgrains occupy an important place in the family budget of a large section of the population in India. Hence, a certain minimum supply of foodgrains at reasonable prices constitutes the rock-bottom of Government's economic policy. To ensure minimum health and efficiency standards, the prices of foodgrains must be held stable at levels within the reach of the poorer sections of the community.

Food Security is one of the major components of social security. It consists of ensuring: (a) that food is available at all times, (b) that all persons have means of and access to it, (c) that it is nutritionally adequate in terms of quantity, quality and variety, and (d) that it is acceptable within the given culture. There are three elements in the above definition: availability, access and suitability.

In recent years, nutrition has been considered as part of food security, and is therefore, referred to as Food and Nutrition Security.

13.1 Food Subsidy

The difference between per quintal economic cost and per quintal Central Issue Price (CIP) gives the quantum of per quintal food subsidy.

Food subsidy is designed to help the producers (farmers) and the consumers of cereals (wheat and rice). The Food Corporation of India procures foodgrains from the market at prices (support prices) fixed by the Government. To these prices are added the handling costs (transportation, storage etc.) to arrive at the economic cost of procuring foodgrains. The procured foodgrains are then released to the public through the public distribution system (PDS). The issue price of foodgrains is less than the economic cost to the Government. The difference between the two is reimbursed to the Food Corporation of India as subsidy. The major determinants of food subsidy are: (a) cost of procurement, (b) storage and distribution, (c) foodgrain stocks, and (d) issue price of cereals.

The basic purpose of food subsidy is to help the weaker sections of population to obtain cereals at reasonable prices. Presently, every citizen of India, irrespective of his economic circumstances, is entitled to draw subsidised items (cereals, sugar, and kerosene) from fair price shops. This is also true in case of subsidised educational and medical facilities. There is hardly any justification for this non-discriminatory treatment of every section of society and some eligibility criterion based on income needs to be fixed. If the cut-off income level is kept low, it will exclude a large section of deserving population. A high cut-off level will have marginal effect. The administrative and enforcement costs of implementing such measures should also be borne in mind.

Producers and consumers and within this group the vulnerable sections of the society are the major beneficiaries of food subsidy. The subsidy incurred on the supply of foodgrains through the PDS at below FCI's economic cost constitutes the consumer subsidy while the producer subsidy is the direct offshoot of the price support based procurement operations of the Government. The producer subsidy together with the cost of maintaining the buffer stock accounts for the cost of buffer stock operations. The consumer subsidy together with the buffer carrying cost constitutes the food subsidy.

The food subsidy bill has increased from year to year in recent times. Though pruning of the existing subsidy level is imperative and could be done by reducing operational inefficiency, the interests of the poor also have to be safeguarded. The surplus stocks of foodgrains with the government provide a vital resource for providing income support to the poor and the vulnerable. Better targeting of subsidies is now beginning to be visible.

Outlining its policy on food subsidy, the Ninth Five Year Plan (1997-2002) observed, "Self-sufficiency in foodgrains for the country as a whole does not necessarily imply food and nutrition security for all. Making food available through the PDS at affordable prices has been a key element of our food security system. However, untargeted PDS has resulted in a steady rise of budgetary food subsidy. During the Ninth Plan subsidised foodgrains is proposed to be targeted only to people below the poverty line so as to ensure that budgetary subsidies reach the needy and become sustainable". [1]

India is not unique in providing either producer subsidies or consumer subsidies in the foodgrains sector. Several countries, including the developed ones, provide subsidies in the area of agriculture and allied operations at levels that are fairly high compared to that in India. In some developed countries, such subsidies which are mainly for the producers, are several times higher than that in India.

The FCI issues foodgrains to the State Governments at a uniform Central Issue Price (CIP) which is considerably lower than the economic cost incurred by the Central Government by way of procurement, storage, transport and distribution. The difference between the economic cost and the CIP is called the consumer subsidy. Since the FCI maintains a large buffer stock of foodgrains, it entails a substantial carrying cost. The consumer subsidy and the carrying cost together add up to the total food subsidy which is borne by the Central Government. It is an important item of revenue expenditure of the Government as shown in its annual budget.

13.2 Public Distribution System (PDS)

Food security is one of the major components of social security. There is enough food available in India. What is required is a well-organised public distribution system. Efforts have been made to streamline the PDS through the introduction of the

Targeted Public Distribution System (TPDS) in June 1997. This system follows a two-tier subsidised pricing structure for families below poverty line (BPL) and for those above poverty line (APL). BPL population receives rice and wheat at a much lower price (hence highly subsidised) whereas APL population is supplied at a price which is much higher and closer to the economic cost. The identification of the poor under the scheme is done by the States.

PDS is the cornerstone of Government's price policy and food security system in India. It ensures availability of certain essential commodities (sugar, kerosene, rice and wheat) at affordable prices, especially for the poor. Through its agency the Food Corporation of India (FCI), the Government procures and stocks foodgrains, which are released every month for distribution through the PDS network across the country.

These commodities are distributed to the public through a network of fair price shops (FPS). In addition to this, the system of procurement is also used by the Government to provide minimum support prices to the farmers in order to stabilise agricultural output and income.

13.2.1 Targeted Public Distribution System (TPDS): A well-targeted and properly functioning PDS is an important constituent of the strategy for poverty alleviation. PDS is operated under the joint responsibility of the Central and State Governments.

The Central Government takes the responsibility for procurement, storage, transportation and bulk allocation of foodgrains, at subsidized prices. The responsibility of distribution to consumers including target groups through a network of fair price shops rests with the State Governments.

TPDS was introduced in 1997 in order to achieve better targeting of food subsidy. Under the TPDS, a dual price mechanism for above poverty line (APL) and below poverty line (BPL) consumers prevails. The full economic cost of foodgrains is recovered from the APL consumers while foodgrains are sold at half the economic cost to BPL consumers.

Criticising the present system of differential PDS pricing,

Mid-term Appraisal of Tenth Five Year Plan (June 2005), observed, "The present system of differential PDS pricing, with very low prices for BPL consumers, is a highly inefficient way of serving the equity objective. There are heavy leakages of as much as 55 percent according to a recent Planning Commission study. The system also distorts incentives for grain producers in non-surplus areas where FCI procurement is poor or non-existent, because it depresses grain prices below the MSP. With the Food for Work Programme in place and the expansion of Mid-Day Meals and the universalisation of Integrated Child Development Services (ICDS), there is a strong case for moving to uniform PDS pricing.

In other words, the PDS, should not be viewed as a poverty reducing instrument as much as an instrument for protecting the common man (including the poor) by stabilising issue prices at a level which may imply only a limited subsidy but which insulates the consumer from sudden increases in prices due to scarcity. The procurement side of the operation should continue to aim at stabilising MSP reasonably above costs of production. Procurement support should also be extended to cover the entire country.

PDS pricing is a sensitive issue, but the proposed change is a logical consequence of the adoption of other schemes aimed at poverty alleviation. It needs to be implemented in parallel with the expansion of other social safety net schemes. The resources saved by moving towards a unified issue price should be directed to expand other poverty reducing programmes, including especially the FFW.

The urban poor are not covered by the Food for work Programme and a case can be made that they need continued subsidy benefits through the PDS. This could be attempted through a system of smart cards. A smart card may be charged with the entitlement of the person who can buy ration commodities from any trader who is linked to the smart card system. The price difference can be automatically transferred to the traders account when the holder makes a purchase". [2]

13.3 Direct Benefit Transfer (DBT)

PDS is a food security programme in India. However, it suffers from various inefficiencies in the sense that a large share of public spending on the PDS does not reach intended beneficiaries.

DBT in lieu of subsidized food has emerged as a leading policy alternative. DBT has the following advantages:

1. Monthly transfers into bank accounts of beneficiaries can cut administrative costs and leakages.
2. Beneficiaries can purchase food of their choice.

There are, however, some disadvantages:

1. Value of transfers may be inadequate, especially if they are not indexed to market prices and inflation.
2. Access to banks/ATMs and markets may vary across locations.
3. Recipients may use cash for non-food items, negating the purpose of subsidy

13.3.1 Nandan Nilekani Task Force: Task Force on an IT Strategy for PDS and an Implementable Solution for the Direct Transfer of Subsidy for Food and Kerosene (Chairman: Nandan Nilekani) was constituted by the Planning Commission to recommend an IT strategy for PDS reform and suggest a solution for direct transfer of subsidies on kerosene, LPG, and fertilizer to the intended beneficiaries. The Terms of Reference of the Task Force were as follows:

1. To identify and suggest required changes in the existing systems, processes and procedures.
2. To suggest IT frameworks and supply chain management.
3. To recommend institutional mechanisms to implement IT strategy for the PDS.
4. To examine and suggest an implementable solution for direct transfer of subsidies on food and kerosene to intended beneficiaries with the use of Aadhaar (Unique Identification Numbers), Aadhaar-enabled transactions, and Aadhaar authentication infrastructure.

The Task Force submitted its report in October 2011 and

made the following main recommendations:

1. Set up a strong, robust IT infrastructure backbone to reform the functioning of PDS, which would be an incentive-based system for all stakeholders.
2. End-to-end computerization of PDS across the country and provision of a token-agnostic technology solution that can accept physical coupons, smartcards, electronic coupons, and facilitate direct cash transfers.
3. PDS Network (PDSN), as the National Information Utility (NIU) to be the common software platform for all States, to implement and operate the IT infrastructure for PDS. PDSN as the technology back office would manage all IT operations related to PDS with focus on supply chain management to address leakages, real time fraud analytics, entitlement portability and transparent grievance redressal channel.
4. Aadhaar (UIN) to be used in PDS to simplify ration card registration, cleaning up the beneficiary database; State Governments can use Aadhaar Payments Bridge and Aadhaar-enabled Payment Systems to channel subsidy funds for approved commodities to Aadhaar-enabled Bank Accounts.
5. Provision of maximum choice to the beneficiaries in terms of location, mix of commodities, convenient quantities and in any number of instalments; and choice to purchase commodities or receive a direct transfer of subsidy.
6. Organizational structure to operationalise the PDS to consist of a Governing Board appointed by the shareholders of PDSN which includes Government of India and other stakeholders with the Chairman of the Board appointed by Government of India. The CEO of PDSN would be selected through an open selection process by the Board.
7. Set up a Core Subsidy Management System (CSMS) for direct transfer of subsidies on kerosene, LPG, and fertilizer through Aadhar-enabled Bank Account (AEBA) to facilitate

robust identification of the beneficiary. The CSMS would support all forms of direct transfers of subsidies such as non-cash transfers, conditional cash transfers, direct cash transfers etc. CSMS would be responsive to the needs of beneficiaries, provide increased transparency, grievance redressal and real time transfer of funds.

8. Fertilizers movement and sale at market price, with reimbursement of subsidy directly to the beneficiary, to reduce the incentive for pilferage due to two prices of the same commodity.

However, it has been found that PDS has failed in large parts of the country, and that it needs to be restructured to be an effective tool of food security. To quote, "The primary motivation for reform originates in the size of the food subsidy bill, even as a proportion of GDP. With escalating economic cost and poor targeting, the food subsidy bill has reached a level that is a significant proportion of the total government expenditure. Further, it also restrains the process of crop diversification". [3]

13.4 Other Food Security Measures

13.4.1 Pradhan Mantri Garib Kalyan Anna Yojana (PMGKAY): To ameliorate the hardships faced by the poor due to economic disruption caused by Covid-19 Pandemic, the Government launched PMGKAY initially for the period from April 2020 to June 2020. However, keeping in view the need for continuous support to the poor and the needy, the scheme was extended and implemented in various phases. Phase V of PMGKAY covered the period December 2021 to March 2022. Under the scheme, 5 kg of additional foodgrains per person per month was provided free of cost to NFSA beneficiaries in all the phases.

13.4.2 One Nation One Ration Card: Under the scheme Integrated Management of Public Distribution System which was started during 2018-19 and 2019-20, One Nation One Ration Card (ONORC) System has been launched. The validity of the scheme was extended to March 31, 2023 from the existing March 31, 2022. Through this system migratory beneficiaries shall be able to access their food security entitlements from any fair price shop (FPS) of their choice by using their same ration card after biometric/Aadhaar authentication on electronic Point of Sale (ePoS) devices at the FPS.

13.4.3 Open Market Sale Scheme: In addition to maintaining buffer stocks and for making a provision for meeting the requirement of the Targeted Public Distribution System (TPDS) and other welfare schemes, Food Corporation of India (FCI) on the instructions from the Government sells excess stocks out of Central Pool through Open Market Sale Scheme (Domestic) in the open market from time to time at pre-determined prices called reserve prices. Under it, a special dispensation for supply of foodgrains to all the charitable or non-governmental organizations etc. engaged in relief or running community kitchens for migrant labourers/vulnerable groups due to the Covid-19 lockdown condition was introduced on April 8, 2020.

Under this scheme, wheat at the uniform rate of ₹ 21 per kilogram and rice at the uniform rate of ₹ 22 per kilogram are issued to charitable institutions/NGOs. There is no upper limit of allocation of foodgrains to each of such organizations from any FCI depot. This special dispensation was initially till June 2020 which was extended for rest of the year 2020-21 at the same rate, terms and conditions. In view of resurgence of Covid pandemic, the said special dispensation was further extended till March 31, 2022 or till further order, whichever is later, at the same rate, terms and conditions.

To sum up, PDS is recognised as a permanent feature of the strategy to control prices, reduce fluctuations and achieve an equitable distribution of essential goods. An efficient public distribution system requires a nexus between production, procurement, transportation, storage, and distribution of the selected commodities.

The working of the PDS is periodically reviewed in

consultation with the State Governments and corrective measures are taken from time to time to improve the supply of various essential commodities to the consumers.

The main challenges in this regard are to improve PDS penetration and reduce leakages. The former is the responsibility of the State governments, and barring moral suasion, the Centre can do little under the present system.

Endnotes

1. Government of India, Planning Commission, *Ninth Five Year Plan* (1997-2002), Volume II, p. 2.
2. Government of India, Planning Commission, *Mid-term Appraisal of Tenth Five Year Plan*, June 2005, pp. 6-7.
3. Government of India, Ministry of Finance, *Central Government Subsidies in India*, December 2004, p. 9.

14

Agricultural Exports and Imports

14.1 Agricultural Exports

Marine products, rice, wheat, sugar, oil meals, tea, coffee, cashew and spices are the prominent products of India's agriculture exports. Meat and meat preparations, fruits and vegetables and processed fruits and vegetables have recently shown strong growth. Despite the advantage of diverse agro-climatic conditions, enabling production of a great variety of products in various seasons, India's exports potential has not yet been adequately addressed. Main reasons for this are the following.

1. Poor export infrastructure.
2. Low level of agriculture product grading.
3. Lack of quality control.
4. Poor branding and packaging.

Infrastructure specific to agriculture exports such as storage, and fast track inland and mechanical port handling facilities are also limiting factors.

Almost all agricultural products are allowed to be freely exported. Export restrictions were removed on groundnut oil, agricultural seeds, wheat and wheat products, butter, rice and pulses from April 2002. Formation of exclusive agriculture export zones is an important step taken to focus on agriculture diversification, value addition and exports.

14.1.1 Agricultural and Processed Food Products Export Development Authority (APEDA): APEDA was established by the Government of India under the Agricultural and Processed Food Products Export Development Authority Act passed by the Parliament in December 1985. The Act came into effect from February 13, 1986 by a notification issued in the Gazette of India. The Authority replaced the

Processed Food Export Promotion Council (PFEPC).

Headquartered in New Delhi, it is headed by a chairman. It has 12 regional offices including metros like Chennai, Hyderabad, Kolkata, Bengaluru and Mumbai. It is entrusted with the task of promoting agricultural exports, including the export of processed foods in value added form. APEDA has also been entrusted with monitoring of export of 16 agricultural and processed food product groups listed in the Schedule to the APEDA Act. It is actively engaged in the development of markets besides upgradation of infrastructure and quality to promote the export of agro-products.

In its endeavour to promote agro-products, APEDA provides financial assistance to the registered exporters under its schemes for: (a) market development, (b) infrastructure development, (c) quality development, (d) research and development and (e) transport assistance.

During 2009-10, APEDA was empowered by an Act of Parliament to enforce the Intellectual Property Right (IPR) of Geographical Indications (GI) for Basmati Rice.

A. Assigned Functions: In accordance with the Act of 1985, the following functions have been assigned to the Authority.

1. Development of industries relating to the scheduled products for export by way of providing financial assistance or otherwise for undertaking surveys and feasibility studies, participation in equity capital through joint ventures and other reliefs and subsidy schemes.
2. Registration of persons as exporters of the scheduled products on payment of such fees as may be prescribed.
3. Fixing of standards and specifications for scheduled products for thc purposc of exports.
4. Carrying out inspection of meat and meat products in slaughter houses, processing plants, storage premises, conveyances or other places where such products are kept or handled for the purpose of ensuring the quality of such products.

5. Improvement of packaging of the scheduled products.
6. Improvement of marketing of the scheduled products outside India.
7. Promotion of export-oriented production and development of the scheduled products.
8. Collection of statistics from the owners of factories or establishments engaged in the production, processing, packaging, marketing or export of the scheduled products or from such other persons as may be prescribed on any matter relating to the scheduled products and publication of the statistics so collected or of any portions thereof or extracts therefrom.
9. Training in various aspects of the industries connected with the scheduled products.
10. Such other matters as may be prescribed.

B. Products Monitored: APEDA is mandated with the responsibility of export promotion and development of the following scheduled products:

1. Fruits, vegetables and their products.
2. Meat and meat products.
3. Poultry and poultry products.
4. Dairy products.
5. Confectionery, biscuits and bakery products.
6. Honey, jaggery and sugar products.
7. Cocoa and its products, chocolates of all kinds.
8. Alcoholic and non-alcoholic beverages.
9. Cereal and cereal products.
10. Groundnuts, peanuts and walnuts.
11. Pickles, papads and chutneys.
12. Guar gum.
13. Floriculture and floriculture products.
14. Herbal and medicinal plants.
15. De-oiled rice bran.
16. Green pepper in brine.

In addition to this, APEDA has been entrusted with the responsibility to monitor the import of sugar.

14.1.2 Strategy to Increase Agricultural Exports: In a country like India with 121 crore population (Census 2011) and agriculture largely depending on the vagaries of monsoon, any strategy to promote agricultural exports will necessarily have demand and supply factors at its core, with instruments of procurement, storage and distribution to service the same. The periodic and recurrent spurts in the prices of essential commodities do not augur well for exports. It is, therefore, essential to have a clear policy about foodgrains based on the buffer norms and strict implementation of the same. As for the perishable products like fruits and vegetables, the country should have a system whereby critical reserves could be procured and stored at strategic locations by a centralized agency to ensure that any unusual rise in the price of a perishable essential commodity can be offset by prompt delivery of sufficient quantities to control the prices.

Such centrally procured stocks of perishable commodities if unutilised for price stabilization, can then be offloaded in the retail market or exported where possible with or without processing before the new harvest of that product comes into the market. This system will need to be fine-tuned to ensure availability of essential commodities at reasonable prices in the domestic market and at the same time continue with sustainable exports to remain a credible supplier in the international market.

A. Infrastructure and Technology: This kind of centralized procurement and storage will require substantial infrastructure to be built in terms of warehouses, cold storage, reefer vans, food processing plants with provision to press in service special railway rakes for swift distribution in the domestic market and shipment to the exporting ports. Dry port facilities may be created at strategic locations in the growing/processing areas to avoid any delays in handling procedures and pre-shipment inspections etc.

Appropriate schemes can be devised for providing incentives for warehousing in the private sector while Government can create the required infrastructure by going in for common facilities for packaging, creating corridors for perishable commodities and cargo handling centres for perishable commodities at all the airports and seaports.

B. Food Processing and Value Addition: Food processing and value addition will be crucial for any strategy to boost exports of agricultural products.

There is lot of wastage for want of post-harvest and food processing technology. Encouraging development of post-harvest technology and incentivising food processing in the producing areas should be central to any sustainable strategy to boost export of agricultural products from the country. Appropriate schemes can be devised to offer incentives for setting up food processing units in the rural areas which should not only generate employment but also provide platform for value addition and diversification of food products to meet the standards and requirements of the importing countries.

C. Market and Product Development: Any international trade in agricultural and processed food products depends on the international demand and supply situation, availability of the concerned product in the domestic market at reasonable price, health safety and quality standards as may be applicable in the importing countries and price competitiveness. For these reasons, it is important to disseminate information about the quality requirements of major markets, create a network of certifying agencies backed with laboratories manned by trained technicians. Besides, agreements for conformity of standards, standard equivalence and agriculture market access for agricultural products in the focus countries should be encouraged.

India is the home of spices and no other country in the world produces, consumes and exports spices in varied forms and in large volume as India does. The strategy in the spices sector aims at making India the premier supplier of quality spices, spice products and herbs in the global market. The medicinal and nutritional values of tea, coffee and spices should be studied and authenticated through clinical trials and patented for aggressive marketing.

Another focus area is that of natural resource based exports. This category includes agriculture, plantation crops, marine products and iron-ore exports. Revitalizing plantations, enabling a less controlled regime for agriculture, and aiming at greater value addition and processed products would help increase the value of exports.

There is a steadily growing market for processed foods and vegetables, organic agricultural produce, and fresh agricultural produce for retail in supermarkets. The availability of abundant raw material, low-cost labour and the large domestic market provides an opportunity to move up the value chain. There is tremendous potential for exports from this sector. The Government is focusing on this sector with mega food processing parks and cold chain projects to address infrastructure issues.

D. Organic Exports: Promoting organic agri-exports through appropriate policy interventions and setting up credible and up-to-date organic export certification and accreditation programmes has to be expanded, especially in the North-East. Presently, India's export of organic products is miniscule. However, recognising the value of organic agriculture for exports particularly in discerning markets such as EU, US and Japan, it is necessary to promote organic agricultural exports to derive greater market realisation. This sector requires special attention which will include major investment in technical capacities for organic certification, outreach and capacity development in states where the potential for organic agriculture is encouraging. Support for packaging, branding and marketing such products and simplification of procedures should also be prioritised.

E. Plantation Products: The plantations sector directly supports livelihoods of about 18 lakh small growers and more than 33 lakh workers, majority of them resource poor, low income groups, inhabiting tribal and geographically challenging terrain, in a sustainable, eco-friendly manner that supports the tribal social structure. Plantation products, especially spices and tea, being closely and strongly associated with Brand India, help to promote Indian cuisine, lifestyle and exports, and establish a personal recall value amongst consumers in general.

Plantations today face a number of challenges including stagnation in productivity due to the ageing plant material, impact of climate change including pests, scarcity of labour and volatile international prices. Stringent food safety regulations in importing markets and the slow movement from commodity to product and brand exports are also squeezing margins and profitability.

To ensure that plantations remain commercially viable, attract investment and professional talent, it is critical that our tea, coffee and spices exports become more competitive in discerning international markets. In order to do so, the following issues assume importance:

1. Productivity enhancement should be a major goal for all plantation products, particularly tea and coffee. Alongside productivity, expansion of the production area is another important challenge. This is particularly relevant for rubber and spices. Through intensive efforts rubber plantations have expanded phenomenally in Tripura but there is still vast potential to expand rubber plantations in Assam and other states of the North-East.
2. Coffee plantations are adversely affected by pests particularly the stem borer. Effective means of neutralising the impact of this pest should be found through scientific and technological methods and collaborative research.
3. India occupies an important position in exports of all the plantation crops. It is the leader in spices, and plays an important role in coffee and tea exports. While tea exports have remained stagnant, coffee exports have grown steadily but need to grow even further. India has essentially remained a bulk supplier of these products thereby not realising the full value of niche products in global markets. Programmes for promoting value added

products of tea, coffee and spices along with support for export after branding of these products should be taken up.

4. Quality compliance is most critical in the case of all these products. A sound technical regulatory infrastructure should be augmented by investment in human resources, infrastructure and equipment.

14.1.3 Agriculture Export Policy, 2018: In December 2018, Ministry of Commerce and Industry, Government of India announced India's first ever Agricultural Export Policy with a focused plan to boost India's agricultural exports to US$ 60 billion by 2022, thereby assisting the Agriculture Ministry in achieving its target of US$ 100 billion and to integrate Indian farmers and the high quality agricultural products with global value chains and to double India's share in world agriculture. The vision of the Agriculture Export Policy is to harness the export potential of Indian agriculture through suitable policy instruments and to make India a global power in agriculture and raise farmers' income.

A. Elements of Agriculture Export Policy: The recommendations in the Agriculture Export Policy are in the following two categories:

(a) Strategic Measures: These include the following:

1. Policy initiatives.
2. Infrastructure and logistics support.
3. Holistic approach to boost exports.
4. Greater involvement of State Governments in agriculture exports.

(b) Operational Measures: These include as under:

1. Focus on clusters.
2. Promoting value added exports.
3. Marketing and promotion of Brand India.
4. Attract private investments into production and processing.
5. Establishment of strong quality regimen.
6. Research and Development.
7. Miscellaneous.

14.1.4 Russia-Ukraine Conflict and Wheat Exports

from India: After rattling the world for almost two years, the Covid pandemic started abating in early 2022 and countries around the world gradually lifted restrictions to restart their economies. However, global economy faced another round of disruptions and dislocations when Russia invaded Ukraine on February 24, 2022.

Ukraine's wheat exports plunged after the Russian invasion. The cost of wheat-related products (like bread and pasta) rose as wheat prices soared on world commodity markets. That came as the conflict cut-off supplies from Ukraine, a major producer of cereals such as maize and wheat. Rising food prices, along with a jump in the cost of energy, pushed up inflation around that world.

India was bullish about increasing the country's wheat exports to meet the surge in global demand. Although India is the world's second biggest wheat producer, it has not previously been a major exporter as most of its crop is sold in the domestic markets.

Wheat shipments from India totalled 7.85 million tonnes in 2021-22, surpassing the target of 7.00 million tonnes and indicating robust exports in the 2022-23. India's wheat exports were 2.10 million tonnes in 2020-21.

However, wheat exports were banned when domestic prices of the commodity started rising. Still the Government of India assured the world community that it would allow exports backed by letters of credit that have already been issued, and to countries that request supplies to meet their food security needs. Government officials also said the ban was not permanent and could be revised.

To sum up, framing policies for the export of agricultural products involves consultations and consensus building with several stakeholders including various Ministries/Departments of the Government of India, State Governments and other organizations. Important considerations while framing a trade policy for agricultural products are as follows:

1. Stocks available in the country.

2. Food security concerns.
3. Domestic price situation.
4. Ensuring remunerative prices for growers.
5. Price competitiveness in the international market.

Production, marketing and pricing policies adopted by major producers of like products or substitutes also influence the export potential of agricultural products. Climatic factors have also become increasingly relevant in this matter.

While India is now a significant supplier of agro products to the world, these remain largely confined to commodities such as cereals, groundnut, castor oil, oil meals, guar gum etc. of which surpluses are limited. It is recognised that while supply side issues need to be actively addressed, there should be a shift in focus towards processed and value added exports and niche products such as organic, culinary herbs and herbal products. A range of facilities and infrastructure on the post-harvest front are needed:

1. Cold chain facilities and transport logistics from the farm to the ports and airports.
2. Silos with temperature control mechanisms to preserve the quality of produce.
3. State-of-the-art pack houses with complete cold chain arrangements.
4. Integrated post harvest facilities and centres for perishable cargo with uninterrupted power supply and connection to National Highways.

The discord between production and exports is evident in the agricultural sector. With rise in incomes and convergence in global consumption patterns for processed foods, India's inability to meet this change in demand for agricultural products has resulted in a continued focus on the export of food commodities like rice and wheat. The opportunities for developing value added exports of cereals, fruits and vegetables, meat and meat products have not been effectively seized.

14.2 Agricultural Imports

In recent years, edible oil, accounting for nearly 60 to 65

percent of the value of total agriculture imports, has become the single largest import item. Raw cashew, nuts (almonds from US) and pulses are among the other dominant agriculture imports. Of late, the share of agriculture imports in total imports of the country has hovered around 4 to 5 percent.

14.2.1 Protecting Domestic Agriculture: Lifting of quantitative restrictions on imports since April 2000 has resulted in import of a number of agriculture products which include fruits, juices, ketchups, meat products etc. Monitoring of 300 sensitive product imports has so far revealed that such imports are limited and, in the aggregate, constitute a small proportion of total agriculture imports. Contrary to concerns in some circles that liberalization of imports—resulting from the lifting of quantitative restrictions on agriculture products—would lead to surge of agriculture imports affecting adversely the Indian farmers, the value of agriculture imports in aggregate terms is quite low.

India has considerable flexibility to counter flooding of the Indian market by cheap agriculture imports through imposition of tariffs (bound rate) under WTO. WTO permissible tariff rates are reasonably high as compared to actual rates. This should provide a fair level of protection. Countervailing duties can also be imposed to counter questionable subsidies given to agriculture products by the exporting countries apart from having the option of acting under safeguard provisions to counter surge of imports.

A Joint Working Group on Agriculture and Marine Products has been set up for facilitating and promoting agricultural trade between India and European Union. The 4th meeting of the Joint Working Group was held in Brussels on May 28, 2010 to discuss agricultural policies, growth in bilateral trade and issues of mutual interest related to agricultural trade.

15

The Three Controversial Farm Laws (Now Repealed)

In the wake of coronavirus pandemic, the Government of India promulgated three Ordinances on June 5, 2020 relating to agriculture.

1. Farmers (Empowerment and Protection) Agreement on Price Assurance and Farm Services Ordinance, 2020.
2. Farmers' Produce Trade and Commerce (Promotion and Facilitation) Ordinance, 2020.
3. Essential Commodities (Amendment) Ordinance, 2020.

   The above three Ordinances were subsequently replaced by Acts of Parliament.

15.1 Farmers (Empowerment and Protection) Agreement on Price Assurance and Farm Services Act, 2020

This Act was passed by the Lok Sabha on September 17, 2020 and by the Rajya Sabha on September 20, 2020. It received the assent of the President on September 27, 2020. It replaced the Farmers (Empowerment and Protection) Agreement on Price Assurance and Farm Services Ordinance, 2020.

It was a dedicated legislation to enable contract farming based on written agreements. It was a law that created a new legal framework for contract farming. It provided for a national framework on farming agreements. It sought to protect and empower farmers to engage with agri-business firms, processors, wholesalers, exporters or large retailers for farm services and sale of future farm produce at a mutually agreed remunerative price.

Contract farming is not new to the country but has seen limited success. The legislation sought to create a new legal framework.

Hitherto, in states permitting the practice, contract farming required registration with the agricultural produce market committees (APMCs) which also acted as dispute settlers. Market fees and levies were paid to these APMCs.

The new law freed up farmers and agri-business companies to engage directly, by passing APMCs. The intent was to make sure that investment flows into agricultural sector. By clearly defining the legal framework, the new law was meant to inspire confidence of both the farmers and agri-businesses.

Once contract farming becomes mainstream, agri-businesses would pool farmers together, invest in their land, provide them with know-how and technology. Contact farming would allow small holders to integrate their production into the supply chains of processing plants.

Under the law, a dispute mechanism could be triggered with the local magistrate who could then call for the dispute to be settled through reconciliation or settle the dispute within 20 days.

The main operative clauses of the contract farming law were that a farmer may enter into a written agreement to supply produce at a future date at a mutually agreed price. The contract could range from 1 to 5 years. The agreement must include the price or a price band. A big advantage of contract farming is that investments in the farm would come from the agri-business company.

15.2 Farmers' Produce Trade and Commerce (Promotion and Facilitation) Act, 2020

This Act was passed by the Lok Sabha on September 17, 2020 and by the Rajya Sabha on September 20, 2020. It received the assent of the President on September 27, 2020. It replaced the Farmers' Produce Trade and Commerce (Promotion and Facilitation) Ordinance, 2020.

This Act was intended to liberate farmers by giving them the freedom to sell anywhere. It permitted intra-state and inter-state trade of farmers' produce beyond the physical premises of Agricultural Produce Market Committee (APMC) and other markets notified under the state APMC Acts. Earlier, agricultural trade could be conducted only in the APMC yards/*mandis*.

It was an Act to provide for the creation of an ecosystem where the farmers and traders could enjoy the freedom of choice relating to sale and purchase of farmers' produce. The Act was envisaged to facilitate lucrative prices for farmers through competitive alternative trading channels to promote barrier-free intra-state and inter-state trade of agricultural goods. The Act also permitted electronic trading of farmers' produce in the specified trade areas.

15.3 Essential Commodities (Amendment) Act, 2020

It was passed by the Lok Sabha on September 15, 2020 and by the Rajya Sabha on September 22, 2020. It received the assent of the President on September 27, 2020. It replaced the Essential Commodities (Amendment) Ordinance, 2020.

The amendment was made with the objective of restricting the conditions on which the government could impose stock limit on agricultural produce. The amendment deregulated key foodstuffs except under extraordinary circumstances. The amended Act required that the imposition of any stock limit on agricultural produce must be based on price rise alone. [1]

The above three legislations were intended to unshackle the agricultural sector in the same way as the Industrial Policy Statement—presented to Parliament on July 24, 1991 by the then Prime Minister Narsimha Rao—which freed the industrial economy of India from the cobwebs of unnecessary bureaucratic controls. In this context, *Economic Survey, 2020-21* observed, "The reforms in the agricultural sector were more overdue than even the labour reforms as the existing laws kept the Indian farmer enslaved to the local *mandi* and their rent-seeking intermediaries. While every other category of producer in India had the freedom to decide where to sell his/her produce, the Indian farmer did not. The local monopolists created by this legal infrastructure enabled the intermediaries to prosper at the cost of the farmer, especially the poor ones without the wherewithal to store their produce. The agricultural reforms enable the farmer to sell where he gets the best deal and thereby enable competition that is sine qua non to create welfare for the small farmer. The reforms in agriculture markets will enable creation of 'One India one market' for agri-products, create innumerable opportunities for farmers to move up the value chain in food processing—from farm to fork, create jobs and increase incomes". [2]

The reforms in the agricultural sector, through the above three legislations, had already started showing results. According to data made available by the Ministry of Agriculture and Farmers Welfare on October 10, 2020, India's exports of agricultural commodities surged by 43.4 percent in the first half (April to September) of 2020-21. While in 2019-20, the total farm exports in April-September period stood at ₹ 37,397 crore, the figure increased to ₹ 53,626 crore in the same period of 2020-21. Increase in agricultural exports was attributable to: (a) increase in supplies (and hence exportable surplus) due to record foodgrains production and (b) deregulation of agricultural markets effected by the promulgation of three Ordinances (later Acts).

However, in view of opposition from certain sections of the farmers, the three farm laws were withdrawn by the government.

Endnotes

1. In this context it is noteworthy that in 2001, a Committee comprising of Central Ministers and a number of Chief Ministers took the view that while the Essential Commodities Act could continue as an umbrella legislation, a progressive dismantling of controls and restrictions was in the best interests of farmers, consumers and traders. Accordingly all restrictions including licensing requirement, stock limits and movement restrictions were dispensed with by the Central Government through the Removal of (Licensing Requirements, Stock Limits and Movement Restrictions) on Specified Foodstuffs Order, 2002 under the Essential Commodities Act, 1955 on February 15, 2002. Dealers were allowed to freely buy, stock, sell,

transport, sell, transport, distribute, dispose etc. any quantity in respect of wheat, paddy/rice, coarse grains, sugar, edible oilseeds and edible oils without requiring any license or permit therefore under any order issued under the Act. State governments would require the Centre's prior permission before issuing any order for regulating, by licences or permits, the storage, transport and distribution of the specified commodities. In August 2006 the Central Government issued an order whereby controls were reintroduced temporarily for a period of six months in respect of wheat and pulses. This order was extended periodically.

Tenth Five Year Plan (2002-07) was also highly critical of the Essential Commodities Act, 1955 which, according to it, is the source of stifling controls and enhanced transaction costs. A large number of permits and licences are required to be obtained from the authorities under the Act, periodic returns have to be submitted and regular inspections are carried out, all of which add to transaction costs. Some notifications under the Act restrict the movement of goods from the surplus states to deficit states. These controls and restrictions, and the constant threat of arrest in case of violations, discourage private companies from producing and distributing essential commodities, thus denying the food sector the benefits of economies of scale and modernisation.

2. Government of India, Ministry of Finance, *Economic Survey, 2020-21*, Volume I, pp. 37-38.

Bibliography

Bibliography

Acharya, S.S. (2006), "Agricultural Marketing and Rural Credit for Strengthening Indian Agriculture", Asian Development Bank, INRM Policy Brief No. 3.

Balakrishnan, M. (2000), "Agriculture and Economic Reforms, Growth and Welfare", *Economic and Political Weekly*, Volume 35, Number 12.

Bhatt, Nitin and Thorat, Y.S.P (2001), "India' Regional Rural Banks: The Institutional Dimension of Reforms", *Journal of Microfinance*, Volume 3, Number 1.

Birthal, P.S., Joshi, P.K., Roy, Devesh and Thorat, Amit (2007), "Diversification in Indian Agriculture towards High-value Crops: The Role of Smallholders", IFPRI Discussion Paper 00727, International Food Policy Research Institute, Washington D.C.

Chand, Ramesh (2016), "E-Platform for National Agricultural Market", *Economic and Political Weekly*, Volume LI, Number 28, July 9.

Chand, R., Saxena, R. and Rana, S. (2015), "Estimates and Analysis of Farm Income in India: 1983-84 to 2011-12", *Economic and Political Weekly*, Volume L, Number 22.

Chand, Ramesh and Srivastava, S.K. (2014), "Changes in Rural Labour Market and its Implications for Indian Agriculture", *Economic and Political Weekly*, Volume XLIX, Number 10, March 8.

Dev, S. Mahendra (2012), "Small Farmers in India: Challenges and Opportunities", IGIDR-Working Paper (WP-2012-014), Indira Gandhi Institute of Development Research, Mumbai.

Dreze, Jean and Sen, Amartya (2002), "India: Development and Participation", Oxford University Press, New Delhi.

Dutta, B. and Ramaswami, B. (2001), "Targeting and Efficiency in the Public Distribution System", *Economic and Political Weekly*, Volume 36, May.

Government of India, Ministry of Agriculture and Farmers Welfare, *Annual Report* (various years).

——Ministry of Finance, *Economic Survey* (various years).

——Ministry of Finance, *Budget Papers* (various years).

——Planning Commission, Plan Documents from First Five Year Plan (1951-52 to 1955-56) to Twelfth Five Year Plan (2012-13 to 2016-17).

Gulati, Ashok (2009), "Emerging Trends in Indian Agriculture: What Can We Learn from These?", *Agricultural Economics Research Review*, Volume 22, July-December.

Hashemi, S.M. (2000), "Micro Credit in Rural Development: Beyond Safety Netting to Poverty Alleviation", CIRDAP Report, July.

Joshi, Sandeep (2000), "Panchayat Raj Institutions and Poverty Alleviation", Rawat Publications, Jaipur.

Kalpana, K. (2005), "Shifting Trajectories in Micro Finance Discourse", *Economic and Political Weekly*, Volume XL, Number 51.

National Bank for Agriculture and Rural Development (NABARD), *Annual Report* (various years).

Niti Aayog (2015), "Raising Agricultural Productivity and Making Farming Remunerative for Farmers".

Patnaik, Prabhat (2005), "On the Need for Providing Employment Guarantee", *Economic and Political Weekly,* January.

Paul, S., Vijayaragavan, K., Singh, P. and Burman, R.R. (2015), "Research Productivity of Agricultural Scientists: Evidences from High Performing and Low Performing Institutes", *The Indian Journal of Agricultural Sciences*, Volume 85 (4).

Pradhan, K.B., Roy, P.K., Sailaja, M.R. and Venkataraman, S. (2000), "Rural-Urban Disparities: Income Distribution, Expenditure Pattern and Social Sector", *Economic and Political Weekly,* Volume 35, July 15.

Prasad, Chandra Shekhar (2005), "India: Economic Policies and

Performance: 1947-48 to 2004-05", New Century Publications, New Delhi.

Pretty, J. (2003), "Social Capital and Connectedness: Issues and Implications for Agriculture, Rural Development and Natural Resource Management in ACP Countries", Technical Centre for Agricultural and Rural Cooperation (CTA), Working Document 8032.

Radhakrishna, R., Rao, K. Hanumantha, Ravi, C., Reddy, Sambi B. (2004), "Chronic Poverty and Malnutrition in 1990s", *Economic and Political Weekly*, July 10.

Rajaraman, Indira (2005), "Financing Rural Infrastructure in Developing Countries", *Applied Econometrics and International Development,* Volume 5.

Rao, Hanumantha C.H. (1995), "Liberalization of Agriculture in India: Some Major Issues", *Indian Journal of Agricultural Economics*, Volume 3.

Rao, P. Parthasarathy, Birthal, P.S. and Joshi, P.K. (2006), "Diversification towards High Value Agriculture Role of Urbanisation and Infrastructure", *Economic and Political Weekly*, June 30.

Ravallion, Martin (2000), "What is Needed for a More Pro-Poor Growth Process in India?", *Economic and Political Weekly*, Volume 35, March 25-31.

Ray, R. (2000), "Poverty, Household Size and Child Welfare in India", *Economic and Political Weekly*, September 23.

Reserve Bank of India, *Bulletin* (various issues).

——*Handbook of Statistics on Indian Economy* (various years).

——*Report on Currency and Finance* (various years).

Satyasai, K.J.S. and Bharti, Sandhya (2016), "Doubling Farmers Income: Way Forward", *Rural Pulse*, Issue XIV, March-April, occasional paper, National Bank for Agriculture and Rural Development (NABARD), Mumbai.

Sawant, S.D., Daptardar, V. and Mhatre, S. (2002), "Capital Formation and Growth in Agriculture: Neglected Aspects and Dimensions", *Economic and Political Weekly*, March 16.

Sharma, S.S.P. (2003), "Development Programmes, Environment and Rural Poverty in India", *Journal of Rural Development*, Volume 22.

Subramanian, S. (2011), "Inclusive Development and the Quintile Income Statistic", *Economic and Political Weekly,* Volume 46, January 22.

Suresh, A. (2013), "Technical Change and Efficiency of Rice Production in India: A Malmquist Total Factor Productivity Approach", *Agricultural Economics Research Review*, Volume 26.

Thamarajakshi, R. (1999), "Agriculture and Economic Reforms", *Economic and Political Weekly*, Volume 34, Number 33.

Vaidyananthan, A. (2000), "Indian Agriculture Policy", *Economic and Political Weekly*, Volume 35, Number 10.

Vyas, V.S. (2001), "Agriculture: Second Round of Economic Reforms", *Economic and Political Weekly,* Volume 36, Number 10.

World Bank (2003), "India: Sustaining Reform, Reducing Poverty", A World Bank Development Policy Review, Oxford University Press.

Websites

Ministry of Agriculture and Farmers Welfare
Ministry of Rural Development
Reserve Bank of India
National Bank for Agriculture and Rural Development (NABARD)
NITI Aayog

Index

Index